Carol Hopkins

Civil War Legacies IV

14 Time-Honored Quilts
for Reproduction Fabrics

Martingale®
Create with Confidence

Civil War Legacies IV:
14 Time-Honored Quilts for Reproduction Fabrics
© 2018 by Carol Hopkins

Martingale®
19021 120th Ave. NE, Ste. 102
Bothell, WA 98011-9511 USA
ShopMartingale.com

Printed in China
23 22 21 20 19 18   8 7 6 5 4 3 2 1

Library of Congress Cataloging-in-Publication Data is available upon request.

ISBN: 978-1-60468-880-1

MISSION STATEMENT

We empower makers who use fabric and yarn to make life more enjoyable.

CREDITS

PUBLISHER AND
CHIEF VISIONARY OFFICER
Jennifer Erbe Keltner

CONTENT DIRECTOR
Karen Costello Soltys

MANAGING EDITOR
Tina Cook

ACQUISITIONS EDITOR
Karen M. Burns

TECHNICAL EDITOR
Debra Finan

COPY EDITORS
Melissa Bryan and
Marcy Heffernan

DESIGN MANAGER
Adrienne Smitke

COVER AND
INTERIOR DESIGNER
Regina Girard

PHOTOGRAPHER
Brent Kane

ILLUSTRATOR
Sandy Huffaker

DEDICATION

To my husband, Edward, who has shown great patience throughout my quilting journey, provided moral support and encouragement at just the right times, and mastered the ability to translate my scribbles into pattern illustrations.

What's your creative passion?
Find it at ShopMartingale.com
books • eBooks • ePatterns • blog • free projects
videos • tutorials • inspiration • giveaways

Contents

Introduction

I am heartened by the fact that in the current environment of beautiful, bright, groundbreaking quilt designs from contemporary fabrics, there are still enough quilters interested in re-creating traditional quilts from reproduction prints to warrant the publication of *Civil War Legacies IV*. As in previous books in my "Civil War Legacies" series, I have selected some of my favorite small quilts that incorporate as many different fabrics as possible in small, classic blocks. These are projects that can be made without large investments of time or fabric, and that also provide the opportunity to explore new color combinations and design options.

For me, small scrap quilts also address the worrisome possibility of using up all of a favorite fabric (an ever-growing category filled with many contenders) in one quilt. I ask myself, "What if I might like it better in another quilt?" and thus, often end up not using it in case an idea for that better quilt comes along. And because I do this over and over again, the "save it" pile just keeps growing. Apparently, others have noticed this phenomenon. One evening, as I was turning out the porch light on my way upstairs to bed, I noticed a sticky note posted on the outside window of the front door. I assumed it was a UPS or FedEx delivery notice; however, when I retrieved it, there, in my granddaughter Allie's handwriting, was the message shown at right.

I treasure this adorable note from my granddaughter.

Translation: "Fabric is not available tonight. At 12 we will charge you more. But if you do it tomorrow, it would be cheap." When I asked her what it meant, she said that I had one more night to use what I needed for my quilt and then in the morning she was selling what was left because I had too much fabric!

How do you explain to an eight-year-old that you *need* all of those fabrics to make interesting scrap quilts? I decided to get out some of my quilts to show her how I used little bits of all those different fabrics. We even counted the different pieces together. In the end, she still thought I had too many fabrics, and I still knew that I needed each and every one of them! If you enjoy collecting reproduction prints as much as I do, I'm sure you know what I'm talking about.

I've learned, though, that even better than just collecting and storing these fabrics, is showcasing them in small quilted treasures that allow me to surround myself with lots of the old-looking prints I love. So, pick a pattern from *Civil War Legacies IV*, dig into your "save it" pile, and cut off little pieces of your favorite reproduction fabrics to create one of the 15 small quilts offered here. You'll be happy you did every time you look at the little legacy you've created.

Wedding Bouquet

Wedding preparations by my oldest son, Tim, and his beautiful bride, Sara, inspired the name of this quilt. The multicolored blocks reminded me of rows of garden flowers that might have been used in a Civil War bride's bouquet as weddings became less formal affairs during wartime.

Materials

Yardage is based on 42"-wide fabric.

100 assorted medium or dark scraps (collectively referred to as "dark"), at least 2" × 4" each, for blocks

½ yard of light print for blocks

⅜ yard of olive print for blocks

⅞ yard of large-scale floral for border and binding

1⅛ yards of fabric for backing

35" × 40" piece of batting

To Add Interest

Select only medium and dark prints for the block rectangles. You'll need 100 rectangles, so the more prints, the merrier. Light prints will disrupt the flow of the blocks, so use lights only in the half-square triangles.

Cutting

All measurements include ¼"-wide seam allowances.

From *each* of the dark scraps, cut:
1 rectangle, 1½" × 3½" (100 total)

From the light print, cut:
5 strips, 1⅞" × 42"; crosscut into 88 squares, 1⅞" × 1⅞". Cut in half diagonally to yield 176 triangles (1 is extra).*
1 strip, 1½" × 42"; crosscut into 25 squares, 1½" × 1½"

From the olive print, cut:
5 strips, 1⅞" × 42"; crosscut into 88 squares, 1⅞" × 1⅞". Cut in half diagonally to yield 176 triangles (1 is extra).*

From the large-scale floral, cut:
4 strips, 4½" × 42"
4 strips, 2" × 42"

*See "Efficient Cutting and Piecing" below before cutting the triangles.

Efficient Cutting and Piecing

Layer a green strip and a light 1⅞"-wide strip right sides together and press them with an iron. Cut the number of squares indicated, keeping each pair of squares together. Cut each pair in half diagonally, keeping the triangles together. The triangles will be layered and ready to sew into the half-square-triangle units.

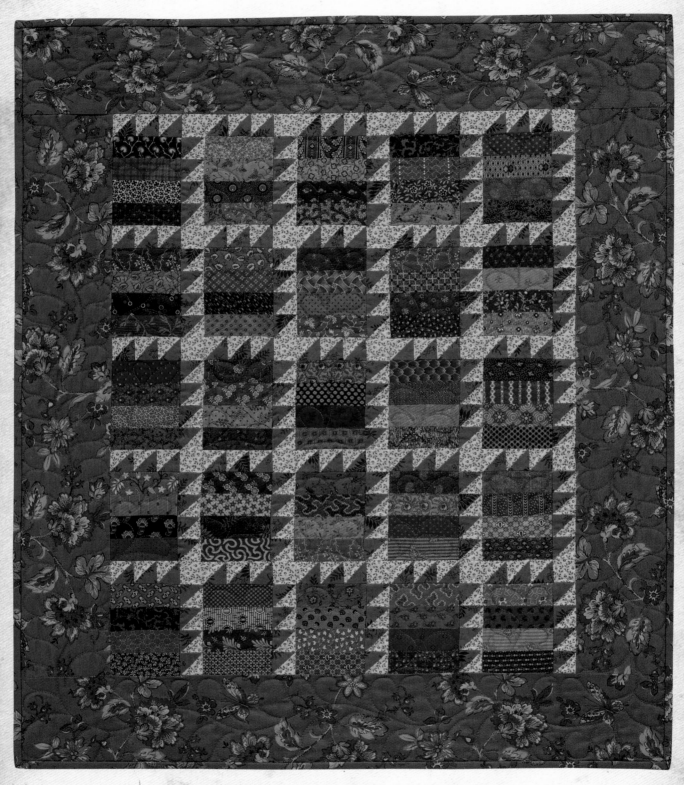

Wedding Bouquet, pieced by Carol Hopkins and quilted by Lisa Ramsey

Finished quilt size: 28½" × 33½" ◇ **Finished block size:** 4" × 5"

Making the Blocks

Instructions are for making one block. Press the seam allowances as indicated by the arrows.

1. Sew together four dark rectangles to make a pieced unit measuring 3½" × 4½", including seam allowances.

Make 1 unit,
3½" × 4½".

2. Sew an olive triangle to a light triangle to make a half-square-triangle unit measuring 1½" square, including seam allowances. Make seven units.

Make 7 units,
1½" × 1½".

3. Sew together four half-square-triangle units as shown. Sew this unit to the right edge of the rectangle unit from step 1.

Make 1 unit,
4½" × 4½".

4. Join three half-square-triangle units and a light square. Sew this unit to the top of the unit from step 3 as shown to complete a block measuring 4½" × 5½", including seam allowances. Repeat to make 25 blocks.

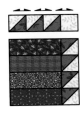

Make 25 blocks,
4½" × 5½".

Assembling and Finishing the Quilt

For more help with any of the finishing steps, go to ShopMartingale.com/HowtoQuilt.

1. Arrange the blocks in five rows of five blocks each. Sew the blocks together into rows and press the seam allowances open. Sew the rows together, pressing the seam allowances open after adding each row.

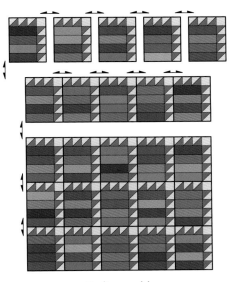

Quilt assembly

2. Measure the length of the quilt top through the center and trim two of the floral 4½"-wide strips to this measurement. Sew the strips to the sides of the quilt top and press the seam allowances toward the border.

3. Measure the width of the quilt top through the center, including the just-added border pieces, and trim the two remaining floral 4½"-wide strips to this measurement. Sew the strips to the top and bottom of the quilt top and press the seam allowances toward the border.

4. Layer the quilt top, batting, and backing. Baste the layers together and hand or machine quilt. The quilt shown is machine quilted with a feathered motif in each block, and feathers in the border.

5. Trim the excess batting and backing fabric. Use the floral 2"-wide strips to bind the quilt. Add a hanging sleeve, if desired, and a label.

Beauregard's Best

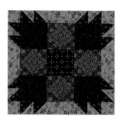

I think Beauregard is a great Civil War–era name. In my imagination, Beauregard is a tall, handsome Southern gentleman. He thinks he's important enough to have a quilt named after himself. Maybe he is. But just in case he's not, it's only a one-block quilt!

Materials

Yardage is based on 42"-wide fabric.

9" × 9" scrap of medium brown print for block

½ yard of light gray print for background

⅓ yard of dark teal print for block and pieced middle border

9" × 9" scrap of red-and-blue print for block

8" × 8" scrap of light teal print for block

½ yard of dark brown print for block and outer border

⅛ yard of red print for inner border

¼ yard of teal-and-red print for binding

1 yard of fabric for backing

31" × 31" piece of batting

To Add Interest

Unify the color palette of the quilt by selecting a background print that includes a color found in one of the darker prints.

Cutting

All measurements include ¼"-wide seam allowances.

From the medium brown print, cut:

8 squares, 2⅜" × 2⅜"; cut in half diagonally to yield 16 triangles*

From the light gray print, cut:

4 rectangles, 2" × 3½"

8 squares, 2⅜" × 2⅜"; cut in half diagonally to yield 16 triangles*

4 squares, 2" × 2"

128 squares, 1½" × 1½"

From the dark teal print, cut:

4 squares, 3½" × 3½"

32 squares, 2½" × 2½"

From the red-and-blue print, cut:

16 squares, 2" × 2"

From the light teal print, cut:

4 squares, 3½" × 3½"

From the dark brown print, cut:

4 strips, 3½" × 42"

1 square, 3½" × 3½" (may be cut from the end of one of the 3½" × 42" strips)

From the red print, cut:

2 strips, 1½" × 42"; cut in half crosswise to yield 4 strips, 1½" × 21"

From the teal-and-red print, cut:

3 strips, 2" × 42"

See "Efficient Cutting and Piecing" below before cutting the triangles.

Efficient Cutting and Piecing

Layer the medium brown and light gray 2⅜"-wide strips right sides together and press them with an iron. Cut the number of squares indicated, keeping each pair of squares together. Cut each pair in half diagonally, keeping the triangles together. The triangles will be layered and ready to sew into half-square-triangle units.

Beauregard's Best, pieced by Carol Hopkins and quilted by Lisa Ramsey

Finished quilt size: 24½" × 24½" ◊ **Finished block size:** 12" × 12"

Making the Center Block

Press the seam allowances as indicated by the arrows.

1. Sew the medium brown and light gray 2⅜" triangles together in pairs to make 16 half-square-triangle units measuring 2" square, including seam allowances.

Make 16 units,
2" × 2".

2. Join two half-square-triangle units and a light gray 2" square as shown to make a unit that measures 2" × 5", including seam allowances. Make four units.

Make 4 units,
2" × 5".

3. Sew together two half-square-triangle units as shown. Make four units measuring 2" × 3½", including seam allowances.

Make 4 units,
2" × 3½".

4. Sew a unit from step 3 to a dark teal 3½" square. Make four units measuring 3½" × 5", including seam allowances.

Make 4 units,
3½" × 5".

5. Join the units from steps 2 and 4 to make four bear's-paw units measuring 5" square, including seam allowances; press.

Make 4 units,
5" × 5".

6. Sew a red-and-blue 2" square to each corner of a light teal 3½" square to make a square-in-a-square unit. Press after adding each square. Make four.

Make 4 units,
3½" × 3½".

7. Sew a light gray 2" × 3½" rectangle to a square-in-a-square unit; press. Make four units measuring 3½" × 5", including seam allowances.

Make 4 units,
3½" × 5".

8. Arrange the dark brown 3½" square with the bear's-paw and square-in-a-square units as shown. Sew the pieces together into rows and then sew the rows together to make a block measuring 12½" square, including seam allowances.

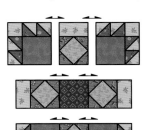 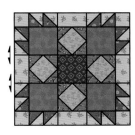

Make 1 block,
12½" × 12½".

Making the Pieced Border

1. Sew a light gray 1½" square to each corner of a dark teal 2½" square to make a square-in-a-square unit. Make 32 units.

Make 32 units,
2½" × 2½".

2. For the side borders, sew together seven square-in-a-square units and press the seam allowances open. Make two borders that measure 2½" × 14½", including seam allowances. For the top and bottom borders, join nine square-in-a-square units and press. Make two borders that measure 2½" × 18½", including seam allowances.

Side border.
Make 2 borders,
2½" × 14½".

Top/bottom border.
Make 2 borders,
2½" × 18½".

Assembling and Finishing the Quilt

For more help with any of the finishing steps, go to ShopMartingale.com/HowtoQuilt.

1. For the inner border, trim two of the red 1½"-wide strips to 12½". Sew the strips to the sides of the 12½" block and press the seam allowances toward the border. Trim the remaining two red 1½"-wide strips to 14½" and sew them to the top and bottom of the unit. Press the seam allowances toward the border.

2. Sew the pieced strips consisting of seven square-in-a-square units to the sides of the quilt top and press the seam allowances toward the just-added borders.

3. Sew the pieced strips consisting of nine square-in-a-square blocks to the top and bottom of the unit and press the seam allowances toward the just-added borders.

4. For the outer border, measure the length of the quilt top through the center and trim two of the dark brown 3½"-wide strips to this measurement. Sew the strips to the sides of the quilt and press.

5. Measure the width of the quilt through the center, including the just-added border pieces, and trim the two remaining dark brown strips to this measurement. Sew the strips to the top and bottom of the quilt and press.

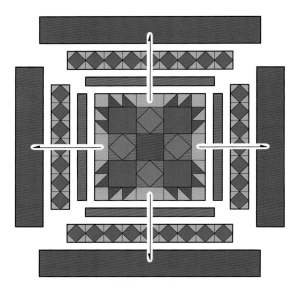

Quilt assembly

6. Layer the quilt top, batting, and backing. Baste the layers together and hand or machine quilt. The quilt shown was machine quilted with pumpkin seed designs in the pieced border and triangles in the center block. The larger squares feature quilted flowers and vine motifs.

7. Trim the excess batting and backing fabric. Use the teal-and-red 2"-wide strips to bind the quilt. Add a hanging sleeve, if desired, and a label.

Blue and Gray Trail

Some of the most dramatic battles of the Civil War were fought from Chattanooga, Tennessee, to the outskirts of Atlanta. This area, in the heart of the war, covered more than 100 miles known as the Blue and Gray Trail. Included in this stretch of battle arenas were Sherman's battle in Atlanta and the Battle of Chickamauga, a site identified as the Confederate soldiers' greatest victory. It is reported that the Tennessee army constructed 300 miles of rifle pits, fired 149,000 rounds of artillery, and spent 22 million rounds of ammunition along this trail.

Materials

Yardage is based on 42"-wide fabric.

5 assorted gray scraps, at least 8" × 11" each, for blocks
9 assorted blue scraps, at least 9" × 11" each, for blocks and pieced inner border
9" × 11" scrap of cream print for blocks
⅓ yard of tan print for blocks and pieced inner border
⅔ yard of gray paisley for outer border and binding
1 yard of fabric for backing
33" × 33" piece of batting

To Add Interest

Select a variety of blue and gray prints so that the blocks look scrappy yet remain close in color and value.

Cutting

All measurements include ¼"-wide seam allowances.

From *each* of the gray scraps, cut:
4 squares, 2½" × 2½" (20 total)
8 squares, 1⅞" × 1⅞"; cut in half diagonally to yield 16 triangles (80 total)

From *each* of 5 blue scraps, cut:
1 square, 2½" × 2½" (5 total)
8 squares, 1⅞" × 1⅞"; cut in half diagonally to yield 16 triangles (80 total)
8 squares, 1½" × 1½" (40 total)

From *each of 4* blue scraps, cut:
1 square, 2½" × 2½" (4 total)
8 squares, 1½" × 1½" (32 total)
4 squares, 1⅞" × 1⅞"; cut in half diagonally to yield 8 triangles (32 total)

From the cream scrap, cut:
20 squares, 1⅞" × 1⅞"; cut in half diagonally to yield 40 triangles

From the tan print, cut:
2 strips, 2½" × 42"; crosscut into 32 squares, 2½" × 2½"
2 strips, 1⅞" × 42"; crosscut into 36 squares, 1⅞" × 1⅞". Cut in half diagonally to yield 72 triangles.
4 squares, 1½" × 1½"

From the gray paisley, cut:
4 strips, 3½" × 42"
3 strips, 2" × 42"

Making the Blue-and-Gray Star Blocks

For each block, pair one blue and one gray print. The same cream print is used for each of the blocks. Instructions are for making one block. Press the seam allowances as indicated by the arrows or as noted in the instructions.

1. Sew a gray triangle to a blue triangle to make a half-square-triangle unit measuring 1½" square, including seam allowances. Make eight. In the same manner, make eight units using the same gray print and the cream print.

Make 8 of each,
1½" × 1½".

Blue and Gray Trail, pieced by Carol Hopkins and quilted by Lisa Ramsey

Finished quilt size: 26½" × 26½" ◇ **Finished block size:** 6" × 6"

2. Arrange the half-square-triangle units as shown. Sew the pieces together into rows, and then sew the rows together to make an hourglass unit measuring 2½" square, including seam allowances. Make four matching units.

Make 4 units,
2½" × 2½".

3. Layer a blue 1½" square on one corner of a gray 2½" square, right sides together. Stitch diagonally from corner to corner as shown; press. Repeat on an adjacent corner of the gray square. Make four matching star-point units.

Make 4 units,
2½" × 2½".

4. Arrange the hourglass and star-point units with a blue 2½" square as shown. Sew the pieces together into rows and then sew the rows together. The block should measure 6½" square, including seam allowances. Make five blue-and-gray Star blocks.

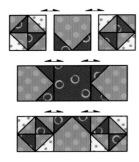 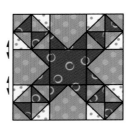

Make 5 blocks,
6½" × 6½".

Making the Blue-and-Tan Star Blocks

Pair a different blue print with the same tan print for each of the four blocks. Instructions are for making one block.

1. Sew blue 1½" squares to two adjacent corners of a tan 2½" square as you did for the blue-and-gray star points. Make four matching units.

Make 4 units,
2½" × 2½".

2. Arrange the star-point units, four tan 2½" squares, and a blue 2½" square as shown. Sew the pieces together into rows and then sew the rows together. Make four blue-and-tan Star blocks measuring 6½" square, including seam allowances.

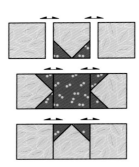 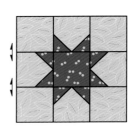

Make 4 blocks,
6½" × 6½".

Making the Pieced Border

1. Join tan and blue triangles to make 72 half-square-triangle units measuring 1½" square, including seam allowances. Press the seam allowances toward the blue triangles.

2. Sew together 18 half-square-triangle units and press the seam allowances open. Make four pieced strips for the inner border.

Make 4 borders,
1½" × 18½".

Assembling and Finishing the Quilt

For more help with any of the finishing steps, go to ShopMartingale.com/HowtoQuilt. Refer to the quilt assembly diagram below as needed for each step.

1. Arrange the nine blocks in three rows of three blocks each as shown below. Sew the blocks together into rows; press the seam allowances open. Sew the rows together, pressing the seam allowances open after adding each row.

2. Sew pieced border strips to the left and right sides of the quilt top, positioning the blue triangles adjacent to the quilt center. Sew a tan 1½" square to each end of the remaining borders, and then sew the pieced strips to the top and bottom of the quilt top, again with the blue triangles adjacent to the quilt center. Press the seam allowances open.

3. For the outer border, measure the length of the quilt top through the center and trim two of the gray paisley 3½"-wide strips to this measurement. Sew the strips to the sides of the quilt.

4. Measure the width of the quilt through the center, including the just-added border pieces, and trim the two remaining gray paisley 3½"-wide strips to this measurement. Sew the strips to the top and bottom of the quilt.

5. Layer the quilt top, batting, and backing. Baste the layers together and hand or machine quilt. The quilt shown is machine quilted with curved lines around each small triangle, and feathers in the border.

6. Trim the excess batting and backing fabric. Use the gray paisley 2"-wide strips to bind the quilt. Add a hanging sleeve, if desired, and a label.

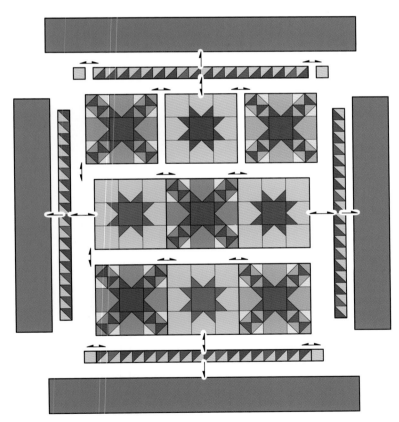

Quilt assembly

Tilly's Basket Sampler

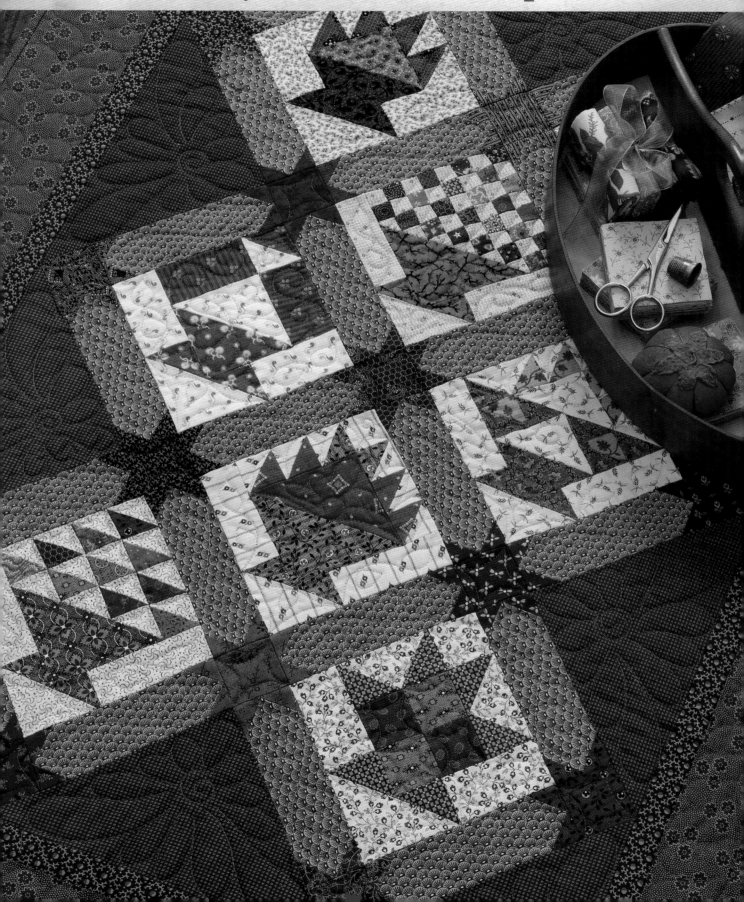

Tilly, a delightful Civil War–era girl's name, seemed to fit the whimsical nature of this basket sampler.

Materials

Yardage is based on 42"-wide fabric. Specific requirements for each block are listed individually.

⅓ yard of pink print for sashing

17 assorted dark scraps, at least 6" × 6" each, for sashing stars

⅜ yard of dark brown check for setting triangles

¼ yard of burgundy print for inner border

¾ yard of brown print for outer border and binding

1¼ yards of fabric for backing

35" × 44" piece of batting

To Add Interest

Choose monochromatic dark prints of the same color for the setting triangles and outer border to frame and highlight the Basket blocks.

Cutting for Setting, Border, and Binding

All measurements include ¼"-wide seam allowances. Cutting instructions are listed individually for each Basket block.

From the pink print, cut:

4 strips, 2" × 42"; crosscut into 24 rectangles, 2" × 5½"

From *each* of the dark 6" × 6" scraps, cut:

1 square, 2" × 2" (17 total)

8 squares, 1¼" × 1¼" (136 total; 40 are extra)

From the dark brown check, cut:

2 squares, 11" × 11"; cut into quarters diagonally to yield 8 side triangles (2 are extra)

2 squares, 8" × 8"; cut in half diagonally to yield 4 corner triangles

From the burgundy print, cut:

4 strips, 1¼" × 42"

From the brown print, cut:

4 strips, 3½" × 42"

4 strips, 2" × 42"

Basket 1

Press all seam allowances as indicated by the arrows.

Materials

1 light scrap, at least 7" × 9"

1 brown scrap, at least 5" × 7"

1 gray scrap, at least 4" × 4"

1 red scrap, at least 4" × 6"

Cutting

From the light scrap, cut:

1 square, 3⅜" × 3⅜"; cut in half diagonally to yield 2 triangles (1 is extra)

2 rectangles, 1¾" × 3"

2 squares, 2⅛" × 2⅛"; cut in half diagonally to yield 4 triangles

1 square, 1¾" × 1¾"

From the brown scrap, cut:

1 square, 3⅜" × 3⅜"; cut in half diagonally to yield 2 triangles (1 is extra)

1 square, 2⅛" × 2⅛"; cut in half diagonally to yield 2 triangles

Tilly's Basket Sampler, pieced by Carol Hopkins and quilted by Lisa Ramsey

Finished quilt size: 28½" × 37⅝" ◇ **Finished block size:** 5" × 5"

From the gray scrap, cut:

1 square, 3⅜" × 3⅜"; cut in half diagonally to yield
   2 triangles (1 is extra)

From the red scrap, cut:

2 squares, 2⅛" × 2⅛"; cut in half diagonally to yield
   4 triangles

Assembling the Block

1. Sew a light 2⅛" triangle to a red 2⅛" triangle to make a half-square-triangle unit. Make four matching units measuring 1¾" square, including seam allowances.

Make 4 units,
1¾" × 1¾".

2. Sew the half-square-triangle units into pairs as shown. Make two units.

Make 1 of each unit,
1¾" × 3".

3. Sew a gray 3⅜" triangle to a brown 3⅜" triangle to make a half-square-triangle unit measuring 3" square, including seam allowances. Arrange the unit with a light 1¾" square and the units from step 2 as shown. Sew the pieces together into rows and then sew the rows together.

 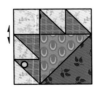

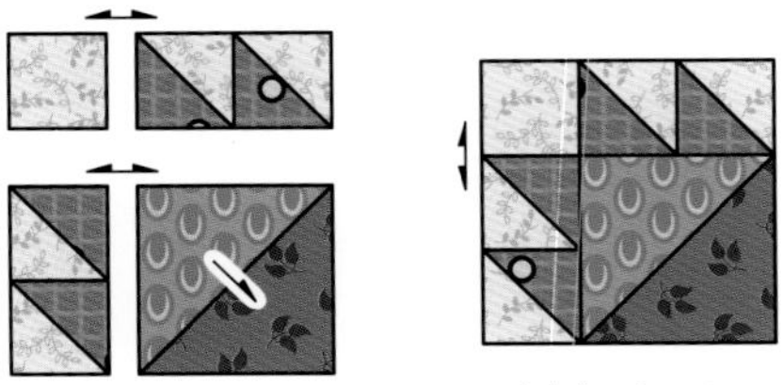

Make 1 unit,
4¼" × 4¼".

4. To make the side units, sew a brown 2⅛" triangle to a light 1¾" × 3" rectangle. Then make a

mirror-image unit, sewing the triangle to the opposite end of a light rectangle.

Make 1 of each unit.

5. Sew the side units to the bottom and right edges of the basket unit as shown; press. Sew a light 3⅜" triangle to the bottom of the basket to complete a block measuring 5½" square, including seam allowances.

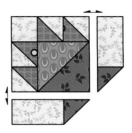 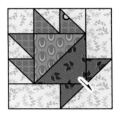

Basket 1.
Make 1, 5½" × 5½".

Basket 2

Make Basket 2 as follows.

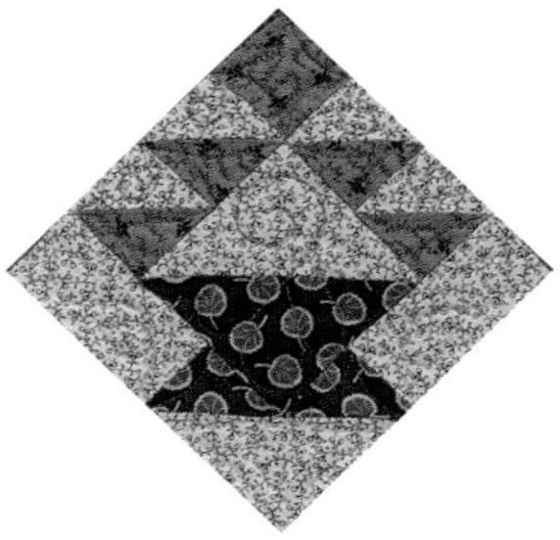

Materials

1 light scrap, at least 7" × 9"
1 black scrap, at least 5" × 7"
1 green scrap, at least 5" × 6"

Cutting

From the light scrap, cut:

1 square, 3⅜" × 3⅜"; cut in half diagonally to yield
   2 triangles
2 rectangles, 1¾" × 3"
2 squares, 2⅛" × 2⅛"; cut in half diagonally to yield
   4 triangles

From the black scrap, cut:

1 square, 3⅜" × 3⅜"; cut in half diagonally to yield
   2 triangles (1 is extra)
1 square, 2⅛" × 2⅛"; cut in half diagonally to yield
   2 triangles

From the green scrap, cut:

2 squares, 2⅛" × 2⅛"; cut in half diagonally to yield
   4 triangles
1 square, 1¾" × 1¾"

Assembling the Block

1. Sew a light 2⅛" triangle to a green 2⅛" triangle to make a half-square-triangle unit. Make four matching units measuring 1¾" square, including seam allowances. Sew the units into pairs as shown.

Make 1 of each unit,
1¾" × 3".

2. Sew a light 3⅜" triangle to a black 3⅜" triangle to make a half-square-triangle unit measuring 3" square, including seam allowances. Arrange the unit with a green 1¾" square and the units from step 1 as shown. Sew the pieces together into rows and then sew the rows together to make a basket unit measuring 4¼" square, including seam allowances.

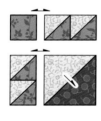 

Make 1 unit,
4¼" × 4¼".

3. To make the side units, sew a black 2⅛" triangle to a light 1¾" × 3" rectangle. Repeat to make a mirror-image unit.

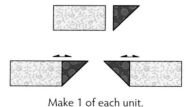

Make 1 of each unit.

4. Arrange the basket unit, the side units, and a light 3⅜" triangle as shown. Join the pieces to complete a block measuring 5½" square, including seam allowances.

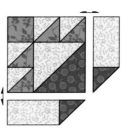 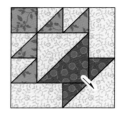

Basket 2.
Make 1, 5½" × 5½".

Basket 3

Make Basket 3 as follows.

Materials

1 light scrap, at least 8" × 10"
1 green scrap, at least 5" × 7"
23 assorted medium or dark scraps (collectively referred to as "dark"), at least 1" × 1" each

Cutting

From the light scrap, cut:
1 square, 2⅞" × 2⅞"; cut in half diagonally to yield 2 triangles (1 is extra)
2 rectangles, 1½" × 3½"
3 squares, 1⅜" × 1⅜"; cut in half diagonally to yield 6 triangles
20 squares, 1" × 1"

From the green scrap, cut:
1 square, 3⅞" × 3⅞"; cut in half diagonally to yield 2 triangles (1 is extra)
1 square, 1⅞" × 1⅞"; cut in half diagonally to yield 2 triangles

From *each* of the dark scraps, cut:
1 square, 1" × 1" (23 total)

Assembling the Block

1. Arrange 23 assorted dark 1" squares, 20 light 1" squares, and six light 1⅜" triangles as shown. Sew

the pieces together into rows and press. Sew the rows together, pressing after adding each row.

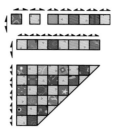

2. Sew a green 3⅞" triangle to the step 1 unit to make a basket unit measuring 4½" square, including seam allowances.

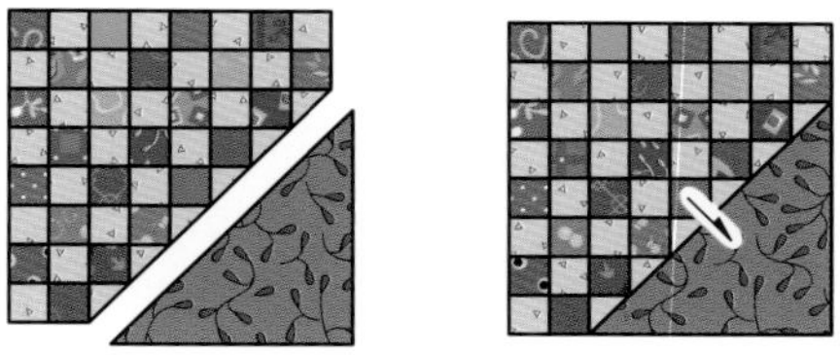

Make 1 unit, 4½" × 4½".

3. To make the side units, sew a green 1⅞" triangle to a light 1½" × 3½" rectangle. Repeat to make a mirror-image unit.

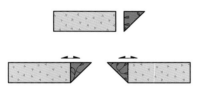

Make 1 of each unit.

4. Sew the side units to the bottom and right edges of the basket unit as shown. Sew a light 2⅞" triangle to the bottom of the basket to complete a block measuring 5½" square, including seam allowances.

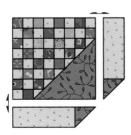 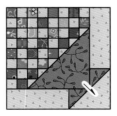

Basket 3.
Make 1, 5½" × 5½".

Basket 4

Make Basket 4 as follows.

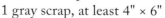

Materials

1 light scrap, at least 6" × 7"
1 brown scrap, at least 5" × 7"
1 gray scrap, at least 4" × 6"

Cutting

From the light scrap, cut:

1 square, 3⅜" × 3⅜"; cut in half diagonally to yield
    2 triangles
2 rectangles, 1¾" × 3"
1 square, 2⅛" × 2⅛"; cut in half diagonally to yield
    2 triangles (1 is extra)

From the brown scrap, cut:

1 square, 3⅜" × 3⅜"; cut in half diagonally to yield
    2 triangles (1 is extra)
1 square, 2⅛" × 2⅛"; cut in half diagonally to yield
    2 triangles

From the gray scrap, cut:

2 rectangles, 1¾" × 3"
1 square, 2⅛" × 2⅛"; cut in half diagonally to yield
    2 triangles (1 is extra)

Assembling the Block

1. Sew a light 2⅛" triangle to a gray 2⅛" triangle to make a half-square-triangle unit measuring 1¾" square, including seam allowances. Sew a light 3⅜" triangle to a brown 3⅜" triangle to make a half-square-triangle unit measuring 3" square, including seam allowances.

2. Arrange two gray 1¾" × 3" rectangles and the units from step 1 as shown. Sew the pieces together into rows and then sew the rows together to make a basket unit measuring 4¼" × 4¼", including seam allowances.

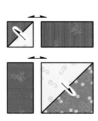

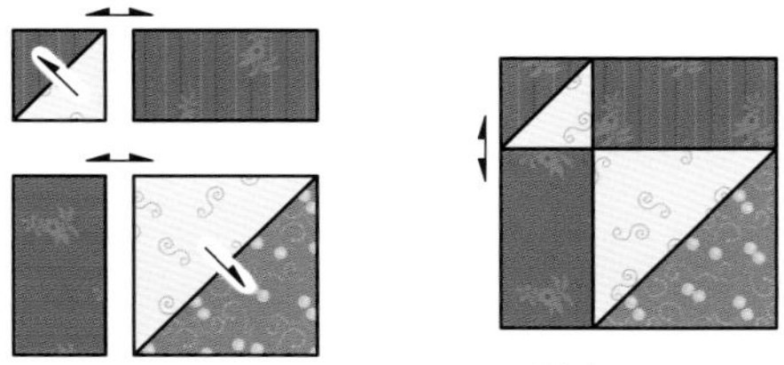

Make 1 unit, 4¼" × 4¼".

3. To make the side units, sew a brown 2⅛" triangle to a light 1¾" × 3" rectangle. Repeat to make a mirror-image unit.

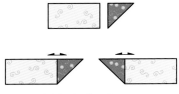

Make 1 of each unit.

4. Sew the side units to the bottom and right edges of the basket unit. Sew a light 3⅜" triangle to the bottom to complete a block measuring 5½" square, including seam allowances.

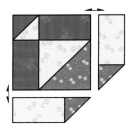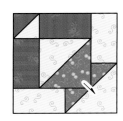

Basket 4.
Make 1, 5½" × 5½".

Basket 5

Make Basket 5 as follows.

Materials

1 light scrap, at least 8" × 9"
1 brown scrap, at least 5" × 8"
1 pink scrap, at least 3" × 7"

Cutting

From the light scrap, cut:
2 squares, 2⅞" × 2⅞"; cut in half diagonally to yield
    4 triangles (1 is extra)
2 rectangles, 1½" × 3½"
3 squares, 1⅞" × 1⅞"; cut in half diagonally to yield
    6 triangles
1 square, 1½" × 1½"

From the brown scrap, cut:
1 square, 2⅞" × 2⅞"; cut in half diagonally to yield
    2 triangles (1 is extra)
4 squares, 1⅞" × 1⅞"; cut in half diagonally to yield
    8 triangles

From the pink scrap, cut:
3 squares, 1⅞" × 1⅞"; cut in half diagonally to yield
    6 triangles

Assembling the Block

1. Sew a light 1⅞" triangle to a pink 1⅞" triangle to make a half-square-triangle unit. Make four matching units measuring 1½" square, including seam allowances.

2. Sew together a light 1½" square, two units from step 1, and a light 1⅞" triangle as shown.

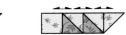

Make 1 unit.

3. Join two step 1 units and a light 1⅞" triangle as shown and press the seam allowances open.

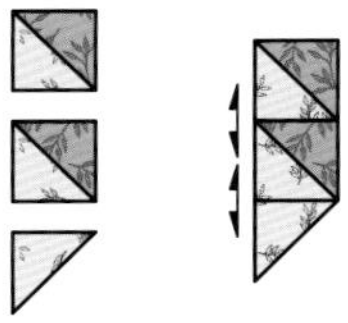

Make 1 unit.

4. Arrange the pieced units with a light 2⅞" triangle as shown. Sew the pieces together into rows and then sew the rows together.

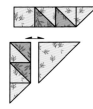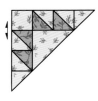

5. Sew a pink 1⅞" triangle to a brown 1⅞" triangle to make a half-square-triangle unit. Make two units measuring 1½" square, including seam allowances. Sew brown 1⅞" triangles to both pink edges of the half-square-triangle units. Trim off the dog-ear points.

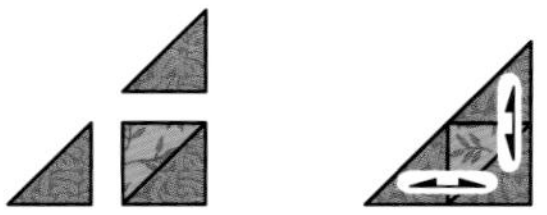

Make 2 units.

6. Sew a light 2⅞" triangle to a brown 2⅞" triangle to make a half-square-triangle unit measuring 2½" square, including seam allowances.

7. Sew the units from step 5 to the light edges of the unit from step 6.

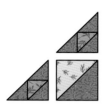

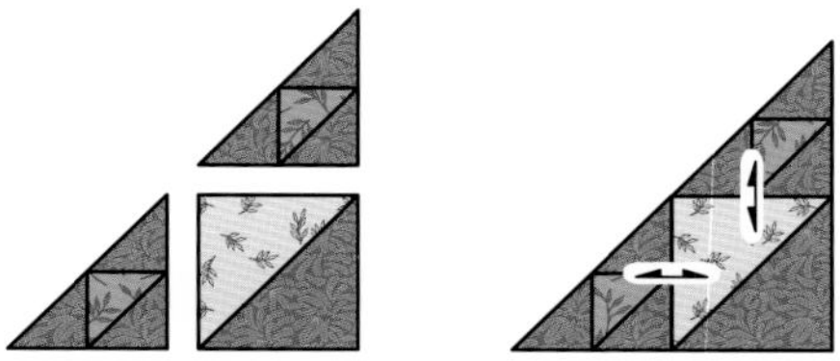

Make 1 unit.

8. Join the units from steps 4 and 7.

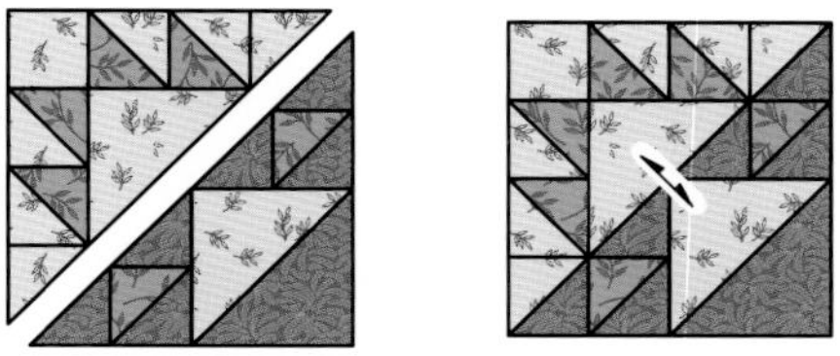

Make 1 unit,
4½" × 4½".

9. To make the side units, sew a brown 1⅞" triangle to a light 1½" × 3½" rectangle. Repeat to make a mirror-image unit.

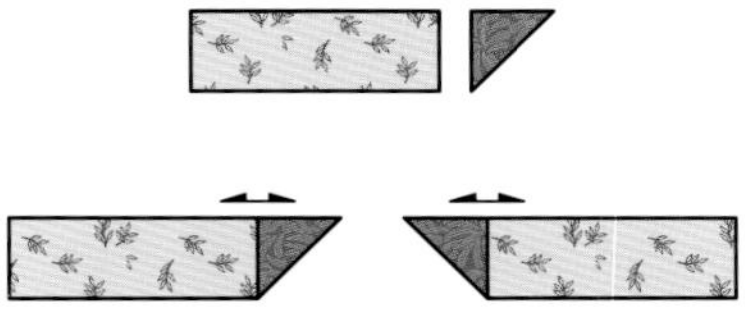

Make 1 of each.

10. Sew the side units to the bottom and right edges of the basket unit. Sew a light 2⅞" triangle to the bottom of the basket to make a block measuring 5½" square, including seam allowances.

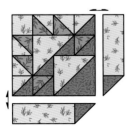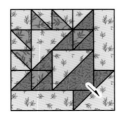

Basket 5.
Make 1, 5½" × 5½".

Basket 6

Make Basket 6 as follows.

Materials

1 light scrap, at least 8" × 8"
1 black scrap, at least 5" × 7"
1 red scrap, at least 5" × 7"

Cutting

From the light scrap, cut:
1 square, 2⅞" × 2⅞"; cut in half diagonally to yield
   2 triangles (1 is extra)
2 rectangles, 1½" × 3½"
3 squares, 1⅞" × 1⅞"; cut in half diagonally to yield
   6 triangles
1 square, 1½" × 1½"

From the black scrap, cut:
1 square, 3⅞" × 3⅞"; cut in half diagonally to yield
   2 triangles (1 is extra)
2 squares, 1⅞" × 1⅞"; cut in half diagonally to yield
   4 triangles

From the red scrap, cut:
1 square, 3⅞" × 3⅞"; cut in half diagonally to yield
   2 triangles (1 is extra)
2 squares, 1⅞" × 1⅞"; cut in half diagonally to yield
   4 triangles

Assembling the Block

1. Sew a red 3⅞" triangle to a black 3⅞" triangle to make a half-square-triangle unit measuring 3½" square, including seam allowances. Press.

2. Sew together light and red 1⅞" triangles to make four half-square-triangle units, and join light and black 1⅞" triangles to make two half-square-triangle units. Each unit should measure 1½" square, including seam allowances.

3. To make the side units, sew together a light 1½" square, two red half-square-triangle units, and

one black half-square-triangle unit as shown. Make a second unit, but omit the light square.

Make 1 unit,
1½" × 4½".

Make 1 unit,
1½" × 3½".

4. Sew the units from step 3 to the top and left edges of the red/black half-square-triangle unit from step 1 to make a unit measuring 4½" square, including seam allowances.

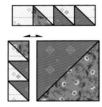 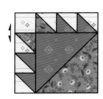

Make 1 unit,
4½" × 4½".

5. To make the side units, sew a black 1⅞" triangle to a light 1½" × 3½" rectangle. Repeat to make a mirror-image unit.

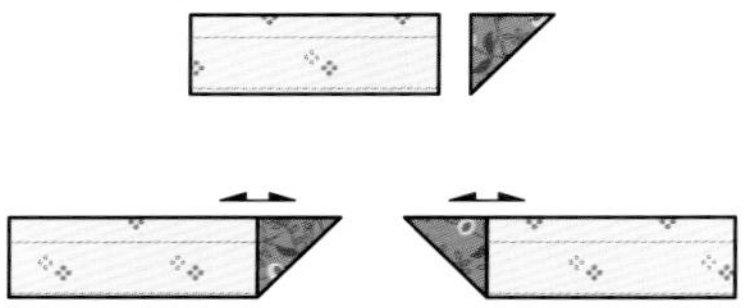

Make 1 of each.

6. Sew the side units to the bottom and right edges of the basket unit. Sew a light 2⅞" triangle to the bottom of the basket to complete a block measuring 5½" square, including seam allowances.

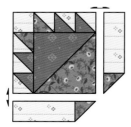 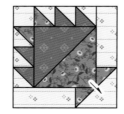

Basket 6.
Make 1, 5½" × 5½".

Basket 7

Make Basket 7 as follows.

Materials

1 light scrap, at least 9" × 10"
1 black scrap, at least 5" × 7"
10 assorted medium or dark scraps (collectively referred to as "dark"), at least 3" × 3" each

Cutting

From the light scrap, cut:

1 square, 2⅞" × 2⅞"; cut in half diagonally to yield 2 triangles (1 is extra)
2 rectangles, 1½" × 3½"
7 squares, 1⅞" × 1⅞"; cut in half diagonally to yield 14 triangles (1 is extra)

From the black scrap, cut:

1 square, 3⅞" × 3⅞"; cut in half diagonally to yield 2 triangles (1 is extra)
1 square, 1⅞" × 1⅞"; cut in half diagonally to yield 2 triangles

From *each* of the dark scraps, cut:

1 square, 1⅞" × 1⅞"; cut in half diagonally to yield 2 triangles (20 total; 10 are extra)

Assembling the Block

1. Sew a dark 1⅞" triangle to a light 1⅞" triangle to make a half-square-triangle unit. Make 10 units measuring 1½" square, including seam allowances.

2. Arrange the units from step 1 with three light 1⅞" triangles as shown. Sew the units into rows and press. Sew the rows together, pressing after adding each row.

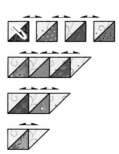 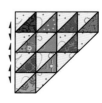

3. Sew a black 3⅞" triangle to the unit from step 2.

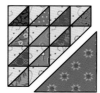

Make 1 unit,
4½" × 4½".

4. To make the side units, sew a black 1⅞" triangle to a light 1½" × 3½" rectangle. Repeat to make a mirror-image unit.

Make 1 of each.

5. Sew the side units to the bottom and right edges of the basket unit as shown. Sew a light 2⅞" triangle to the bottom of the basket to complete a block measuring 5½" square, including seam allowances.

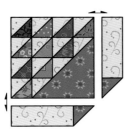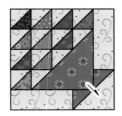

Basket 7.
Make 1, 5½" × 5½".

Basket 8

Make Basket 8 as follows.

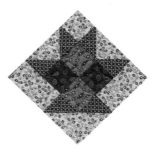

Materials

1 light scrap, at least 7" × 10"
1 blue scrap, at least 5" × 7"
1 brown scrap, at least 3" × 5"
1 cheddar scrap, at least 3" × 5"

Cutting

From the light scrap, cut:

1 square, 3⅜" × 3⅜"; cut in half diagonally to yield
    2 triangles (1 is extra)
4 rectangles, 1¾" × 3"
1 square, 1¾" × 1¾"

From the blue scrap, cut:

4 squares, 1¾" × 1¾"
1 square, 2⅛" × 2⅛"; cut in half diagonally to yield
    2 triangles

From the brown scrap, cut:

2 squares, 1¾" × 1¾"

From the cheddar scrap, cut:

2 squares, 1¾" × 1¾"

Assembling the Block

1. Make a flying-geese unit with two blue 1¾" squares and one light 1¾" × 3" rectangle as shown. Make two matching units.

Make 2 units,
1¾" × 3".

2. Sew two brown 1¾" squares and two cheddar 1¾" squares together to make a four-patch unit measuring 3" square, including seam allowances.

Make 1 unit,
3" × 3".

3. Arrange a light 1¾" square with the flying-geese and four-patch units. Sew the pieces into rows and then join the rows together to make a unit measuring 4¼" square, including seam allowances.

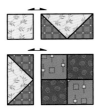

Make 1 unit,
4¼" × 4¼".

4. To make the side units, sew a blue 2⅛" triangle to a light 1¾" × 3" rectangle as shown. Repeat to make a mirror-image unit.

Make 1 of each unit.

5. Sew the side units to the bottom and right edges of the basket unit. Sew a light 3⅜" triangle to the bottom to complete a block measuring 5½" square, including seam allowances.

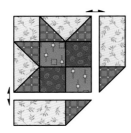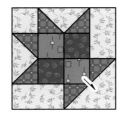

Basket 8.
Make 1, 5½" × 5½".

Assembling and Finishing the Quilt

For more help with any of the finishing steps, go to ShopMartingale.com/HowtoQuilt.

1. Arrange the blocks, sashing rectangles, sashing squares, and setting triangles as shown.

2. Working with one sashing rectangle at a time, sew two 1¼" squares that match the adjacent sashing square to one end of a 2" × 5½" pink rectangle. Repeat on the other end of the same sashing rectangle using 1¼" squares that match the 2" sashing square they touch. Make 24 sashing rectangle units.

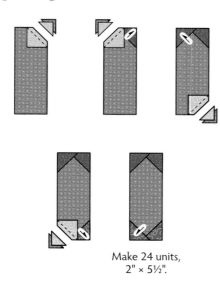

Make 24 units,
2" × 5½".

3. Sew the blocks, sashing rectangles, and sashing squares together into rows as shown.

4. Sew the block rows and sashing strips together and press after adding each row. Add the side setting triangles to the rows; press.

5. Center the brown check corner triangles and sew them to the quilt.

6. Trim and square up the quilt top, leaving ¼" seam allowances beyond the corners of the blocks.

7. For the inner border, measure the length of the quilt top through the center and trim two of the burgundy 1¼"-wide strips to this measurement. Sew the strips to the sides of the quilt top and press the seam allowances toward the border.

8. Measure the width of the quilt top through the center, including the just-added border pieces, and trim the two remaining burgundy 1¼"-wide strips to this measurement. Sew the strips to the top and bottom of the quilt and press the seam allowances toward the border.

9. For the outer border, repeat steps 6 and 7 using the brown 3½"-wide strips.

10. Layer the quilt top, batting, and backing. Baste the layers together and hand or machine quilt. The quilt shown is machine quilted with leaves and scrolls in the blocks, flowers in the side triangles, and feathers in the border.

11. Trim the excess batting and backing fabric. Use the brown 2"-wide strips to bind the quilt. Add a hanging sleeve, if desired, and a label.

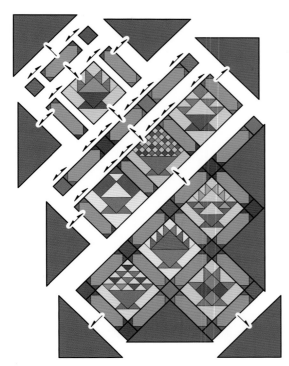

Quilt assembly

Dominoes

While in camp, soldiers spent idle time between battles repairing their uniforms, reading, writing letters, serving guard duty, and playing card games and dominoes. Many soldiers carried small sets of dominoes made of wood, bone, or ivory in their knapsacks or pockets.

Materials

Yardage is based on 42"-wide fabric.

½ yard of brown print for outer border

⅓ yard of dark brown print for binding

¼ yard of red print for inner border

½ yard of beige print for background

66 assorted dark scraps, at least 3¼" × 3¼", for blocks

4 assorted light print scraps, at least 3¼" × 3¼", for blocks

42 assorted light scraps, at least 2" × 2", for blocks

1⅜ yards of fabric for backing

36" × 46" piece of batting

To Add Interest

Break away from boring beige! For the block centers, select a variety of light prints that are darker and more colorful than the print used for the setting rectangles. This subtle strategy will make these little squares dance across your quilt top.

Cutting

All measurements include ¼"-wide seam allowances.

From the brown print, cut:

4 strips, 4" × 42"

From the dark brown print, cut:

4 strips, 2" × 42"

From the red print, cut:

4 strips, 1" × 42"

From the beige print, cut:

3 strips, 4½" × 42"; crosscut into 41 rectangles, 2½" × 4½"

6 squares, 2½" × 2½"

From *each* dark print scrap, cut:

1 square, 3¼" × 3¼"; cut in quarters diagonally to yield 4 triangles (264 total)

From *each* 3¼" light print scrap, cut:

1 square, 3¼" × 3¼"; cut into quarters diagonally to yield 4 triangles (16 total; 3 of each print are extra)

From *each* 2" light print scrap, cut:

1 square, 2" × 2" (42 total)

Dominoes, pieced by Carol Hopkins and quilted by Lisa Ramsey

Finished quilt size: 30½" × 40½" ◇ **Finished block size:** 2" × 4"

Making the Blocks

Press the seam allowances as indicated by the arrows.

1. Choose one set of four matching dark triangles, one pair of contrasting dark triangles, and one light square.

2. Lay out the square and triangles as shown. Sew the pieces into three units; press. Sew the units together; press. The block should measure 2½" × 4½", including seam allowances. Make 42.

Make 42 blocks,
2½" × 4½".

3. Sew two matching dark triangles, one different dark triangle, and one light triangle together as shown; press to make an hourglass unit measuring 2½" square. Make four.

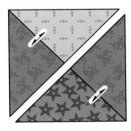

Make 4 half blocks,
2½" × 2½".

Assembling and Finishing the Quilt

1. Arrange the blocks and beige print rectangles and squares in 11 vertical rows as shown. Sew the blocks into rows; press. Sew the rows together; press after adding each row.

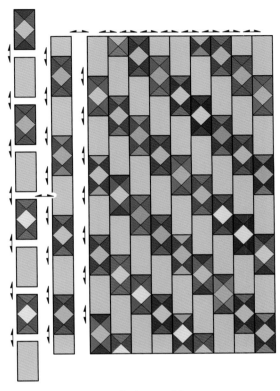

Quilt assembly

2. Measure the length of the quilt top through the center and trim two red strips to this measurement. Sew the strips to the sides of the quilt; press.

3. Measure the width of the quilt through the center, including the just-added border pieces, and trim the remaining red strips to this measurement. Sew the strips to the top and bottom of the quilt; press.

4. Repeat steps 2 and 3 with the brown print strips for the outer border.

5. Use the dark brown print 2"-wide strips to bind the quilt. Add a hanging sleeve, if desired, and a label.

Little Annie

I named this quilt, consisting of two alternating units that form Pinwheel Album blocks, in remembrance of my mother, Anne. Her brother and sisters always called her "Annie."

Materials

Yardage is based on 42"-wide fabric.

⅝ yard of light print for background and inner border

8 assorted light scraps, at least 4" × 6" each, for blocks

8 assorted medium or dark scraps (collectively referred to as "dark"), at least 4" × 8" each, for blocks

8 assorted medium or dark scraps (collectively referred to as "dark"), at least 4" × 6" each, for blocks

8 assorted medium or dark scraps (collectively referred to as "dark"), at least 4" × 4" each, for blocks

¼ yard of black-and-brown print for middle border

1⅛ yards of directional red print *OR* ½ yard of nondirectional red print for outer border

⅓ yard of brown print for binding

1¼ yards of fabric for backing

33" × 43" piece of batting

To Add Interest

Select a nondirectional background fabric that contrasts strongly with the block fabrics to make the interesting shape of the Album blocks stand out. A busy print with a lot of movement, such as flowers or vines, will ensure that seamlines do not detract from the overall design.

Cutting

All measurements include ¼"-wide seam allowances.

From the light print, cut:

1 strip, 3½" × 42"; crosscut into 7 squares, 3½" × 3½" (B)

3 strips, 1½" × 42"; crosscut into 64 squares, 1½" × 1½"

2 strips, 2½" × 42"; crosscut into:
   18 squares, 2½" × 2½" (A)
   6 rectangles, 2½" × 5½" (C)

4 strips, 1½" × 42"

From *each* of the light scraps, cut:

2 squares, 2⅜" × 2⅜"; cut in half diagonally to yield 4 triangles (32 total)

From *each* of the dark 4" × 8" scraps, cut:

4 rectangles, 1½" × 3½" (32 total)

From *each* of the dark 4" × 6" scraps, cut:

2 squares, 2⅜" × 2⅜"; cut in half diagonally to yield 4 triangles (32 total)

From *each* of the dark 4" × 4" scraps, cut:

4 squares, 1½" × 1½" (32 total)

From the black-and-brown print, cut:

4 strips, 1¼" × 42"

From the *lengthwise* grain of the red print, cut:*

2 strips, 3½" ×33"

From the *crosswise* grain of the remaining red print, cut:

2 strips, 3½" × 30"

From the brown print, cut:

4 strips, 2" × 42"

*If you're using a nondirectional print, cut the strips across the fabric width.

Little Annie, pieced by Carol Hopkins and quilted by Lisa Ramsey

Finished quilt size: 27" × 37" ◇ **Finished block size:** 5" × 5"

Making the Blocks

This quilt consists of eight blocks, plus pieced units to complete the design. You need to construct the blocks and determine their position in the quilt before you make the setting pieces so that you can complete the color scheme.

Each block contains five different fabrics. Instructions are for making one block. Press the seam allowances as indicated by the arrows.

1. Sew light 1½" squares to opposite sides of a dark 1½" square. Make four matching units measuring 1½" × 3½", including seam allowances.

Make 4 units,
1½" × 3½".

2. Sew a contrasting dark 1½" × 3½" rectangle to each pieced unit. Make four matching units measuring 2½" × 3½", including seam allowances. Set aside two of these units for the background units.

Make 4 units,
2½" × 3½".

3. Join light and dark 2⅜" triangles to make four matching half-square-triangle units measuring 2" square, including seam allowances.

Make 4 units,
2" × 2".

4. Arrange four half-square-triangle units as shown. Sew the units together into rows, and then sew the rows together to make a pinwheel unit measuring 3½" square, including seam allowances.

Make 1 unit,
3½" × 3½".

5. Arrange a light 2½" A square, two units from step 2, and the pinwheel unit as shown. Sew the units together into rows, and then sew the rows together to make a block measuring 5½" square, including seam allowances. Repeat to make a total of eight blocks.

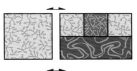 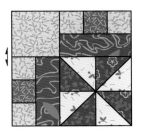
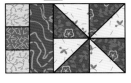

Make 8 blocks,
5½" × 5½".

Assembling and Finishing the Quilt

Press each seam open after sewing. For more help with any of the finishing steps, go to ShopMartingale.com/HowtoQuilt.

1. Arrange the blocks in a checkerboard pattern as shown, making sure all of the blocks are oriented in the same direction.

2. Place the remaining pieced units from step 2 of "Making the Blocks" next to their matching pieced blocks. Starting with the top row and working on one section at a time, remove the first pieced unit from the layout, join it to a light 3½" B square, and press. Join a light 2½" × 5½" C rectangle to the unit, press, and then return the unit to its position in the layout.

3. Following the quilt layout diagram below, complete each background unit using the following light pieces: 2½" A squares, 3½" B squares, and 2½" × 5½" C rectangles.

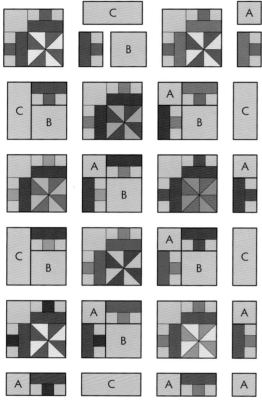

Quilt layout

4. Sew the blocks and pieced background units together in rows; press. Sew the rows together and press after adding each row.

5. For the inner border, measure the length of the quilt top through the center and trim two of the light 1½"-wide strips to this measurement. Sew the strips to the sides of the quilt top.

6. Measure the width of the quilt through the center, including the just-added border pieces, and trim the two remaining light 1½"-wide strips to this measurement. Sew the strips to the top and bottom of the quilt top.

7. For the middle border, repeat steps 2 and 3 using the black-and-brown 1¼"-wide strips.

8. For the outer border, repeat steps 6 and 7 using the red 3½"-wide strips.

Quilt assembly

9. Layer the quilt top, batting, and backing. Baste the layers together and hand or machine quilt. The quilt shown is machine quilted with a pumpkin seed design in the blocks and swirling feathers in the background and border.

10. Trim the excess batting and backing fabric. Use the brown 2"-wide strips to bind the quilt. Add a hanging sleeve, if desired, and a label.

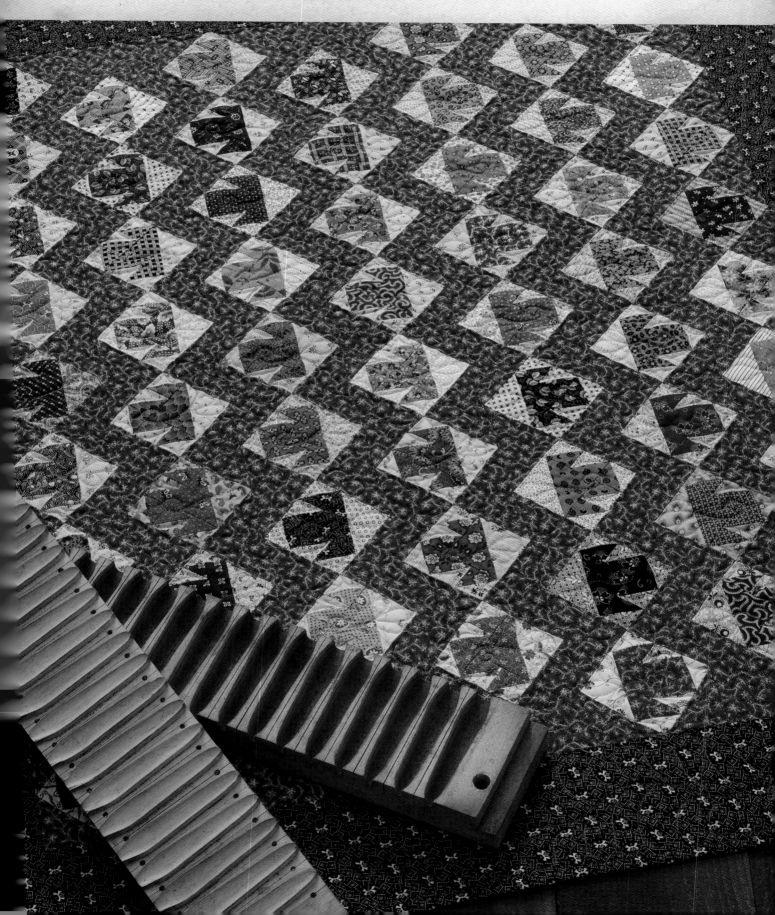

The fife and drum were popular Civil War instruments. Each company of approximately 100 men was assigned two fifers and two drummers, who sounded signals to inform troops of daily activities such as wake-up time, meals, bedtime, and the need to assemble. At times, signals warned of approaching enemies. Additionally, these instruments provided music as the soldiers marched, often to songs from home. This project is a small version of a larger quilt created by an unknown maker in the 1800s.

Materials

Yardage is based on 42"-wide fabric.

60 assorted light scraps, at least 6" × 6" each, for blocks
60 assorted dark scraps, at least 6" × 6" each, for blocks
1 yard of red print for setting triangles
⅞ yard of blue print for border and binding
2¾ yards of fabric for backing*
45" × 53" piece of batting

If your fabric is wider than 42", one length of fabric (1⅜ yards) will be sufficient for the quilt backing.

To Add Interest

Be bold! Include large-scale prints that contain a variety of colors to create visual interest in your quilt.

Cutting

All measurements include ¼"-wide seam allowances.

From *each* of the light scraps, cut:
1 square, 2⅞" × 2⅞"; cut in half diagonally to yield
    2 triangles (120 total; 60 are extra)
3 squares, 1⅞" × 1⅞"; cut in half diagonally to yield
    6 triangles (360 total; 60 are extra)

From *each* of the dark scraps, cut:
1 square, 2⅞" × 2⅞"; cut in half diagonally to yield
    2 triangles (120 total; 60 are extra)
3 squares, 1⅞" × 1⅞"; cut in half diagonally to yield
    6 triangles (360 total; 60 are extra)

From the red print, cut:
5 strips, 5½" × 42"; crosscut into 31 squares,
    5½" × 5½". Cut into quarters diagonally to yield
    124 side triangles.
1 strip, 3" × 42"; crosscut into 8 squares, 3" × 3". Cut
    in half diagonally to yield 16 corner triangles.

From the blue print, cut:
4 strips, 4½" × 42"
5 strips, 2" × 42"

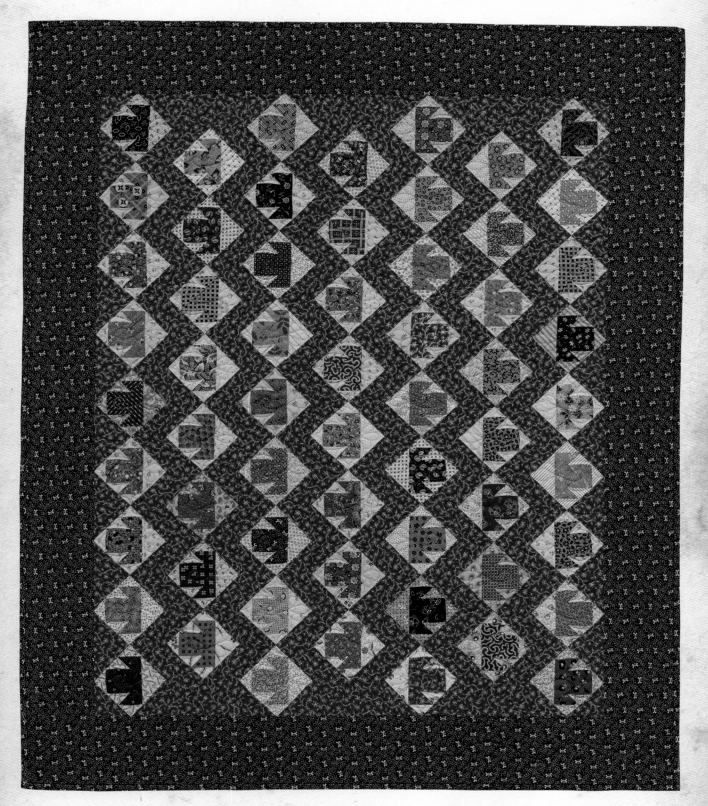

Fife and Drum, pieced by Carol Hopkins and quilted by Lisa Ramsey
Finished quilt size: 38¼" × 46⅝" ◇ **Finished block size:** 3" × 3"

Making the Blocks

Each block contains a light print and a dark print. Instructions are for making one block. Press the seam allowances as indicated by the arrows.

1. Sew a light 1⅞" triangle to a dark 1⅞" triangle to make a half-square-triangle unit. Make five matching units measuring 1½" square, including seam allowances.

Make 5 units,
1½" × 1½".

2. In the same manner, sew a matching light and a matching dark 2⅞" triangle together to make a half-square-triangle unit measuring 2½" square, including seam allowances. Press.

3. Sew two small half-square-triangle units together as shown.

Make 1 unit,
1½" × 2½".

4. Sew three small half-square-triangle units together as shown.

Make 1 unit,
1½" × 3½".

5. Sew the two pieced units to the large half-square-triangle unit as shown to complete a block measuring 3½" square, including seam allowances. Make 60 blocks.

 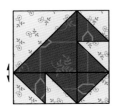

Make 60 blocks,
3½" × 3½".

Assembling and Finishing the Quilt

For more help with any of the finishing steps, go to ShopMartingale.com/HowtoQuilt.

1. Arrange nine blocks, 16 side triangles, and four corner triangles as shown. Sew the pieces into nine diagonal units; press. Sew the units together and add one corner triangle to each end to complete one row A. Press. Repeat to make a total of four A rows that are 4¾" × 38⅝", including seam allowances.

Row A.
Make 4 rows,
4¾" × 38⅝".

2. Lay out eight blocks and 20 side triangles as shown. Sew the pieces into 10 diagonal units. Sew the units together to complete one row B. Press. Repeat to make a total of three B rows that are 4¾" × 38⅝", including seam allowances.

Row B.
Make 3 rows,
4¾" × 38⅝".

3. Sew the A and B rows together, alternating them as shown. Press after adding each row.

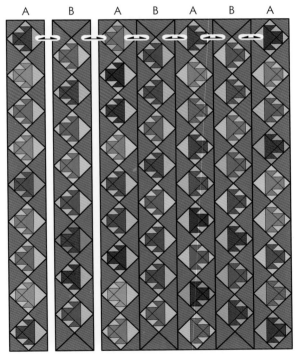

A B A B A B A

Quilt assembly

4. Measure the length of the quilt top through the center and trim two blue 4½"-wide strips to this measurement. Sew the strips to the sides of the quilt and press the seam allowances toward the border.

5. Measure the width of the quilt top through the center, including the just-added border pieces, and trim the two remaining blue 4½"-wide strips to that length. Sew the strips to the top and bottom of the quilt and press the seam allowances toward the border.

6. Layer the quilt top, batting, and backing. Baste the layers together and hand or machine quilt. The quilt shown is machine quilted with a flower and swirl in each block, and a feather vine in the background and border.

7. Trim the excess batting and backing fabric. Use the blue 2"-wide strips to bind the quilt. Add a hanging sleeve, if desired, and a label.

Loreta's Corset

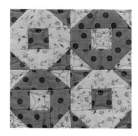

In some of my previous patterns, such as Mary Smith's Dishrag and Lizzie's Tents, I've recounted stories of women who disguised themselves as men so that they could fight on the battlefield. Richard Hall tells the story of Loreta Janeta Velazquez who, in addition to wearing a fake mustache and walking with a practiced swagger, donned a specially designed chain-metal corset to hide her curvaceous body shape. The only problem, Loreta reported in her own memoir, was that because the corset shifted and got "out of order," she was repeatedly stopped and interrogated. Perhaps the chain-metal links looked something like the blocks in this quilt.

Materials

Yardage is based on 42"-wide fabric.

13 assorted dark scraps, at least 6" × 9" each, for blocks

13 assorted light scraps, at least 6" × 9" each, for blocks

⅜ yard of taupe print for setting squares

¼ yard of tan print for inner border

⅝ yard of blue-and-tan print for outer border

⅓ yard of blue print for binding

1⅛ yards of fabric for backing

38" × 38" piece of batting

To Add Interest

Including light prints with undertones of pink, blue, and brown as well as plaids and stripes will create variety in an otherwise uniform block design.

Cutting

All measurements include ¼"-wide seam allowances.

From *each* of the dark scraps, cut:
4 rectangles, 1¼" × 2" (52 total)
2 rectangles, 1¼" × 2¾" (26 total)
12 squares, 1¼" × 1¼" (156 total)

From *each* of the light scraps, cut:
4 rectangles, 1¼" × 2" (52 total)
2 rectangles, 1¼" × 2¾" (26 total)
12 squares, 1¼" × 1¼" (156 total)

From the taupe print, cut:
2 strips, 5" × 42"; crosscut into 12 squares, 5" × 5"

From the tan print, cut:
4 strips, 1¼" × 42"

From the blue-and-tan print, cut:
4 strips, 4" × 42"

From the blue print, cut:
4 strips, 2" × 42"

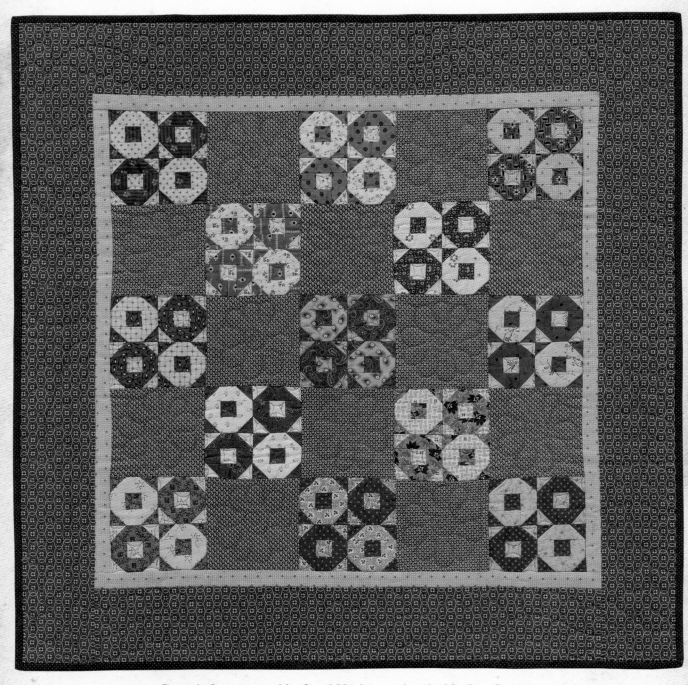

Loreta's Corset, pieced by Carol Hopkins and quilted by Lisa Ramsey

Finished quilt size: 31½" × 31½" ◇ **Finished block size:** 4½" × 4½"

Making the Blocks

Each block contains one light and one dark fabric. Instructions are for making one block. Press the seam allowances as indicated by the arrows.

1. Place a dark 1¼" square on one end of a light 1¼" × 2" rectangle, right sides together. Sew diagonally across the dark square and trim the seam allowance to ¼". Press. Make four matching units.

Make 4 units,
1¼" × 2".

2. In the same manner, sew, trim, and press matching 1¼" dark squares on opposite ends of a light 1¼" × 2¾" rectangle. Make two.

Make 2 units,
1¼" × 2¾".

3. Sew a light 1¼" square to a dark 1¼" square. Sew this unit to one long edge of a unit from step 1 to make a unit measuring 2" square, including seam allowances. Make two.

Make 2 units,
2" × 2".

4. Join the units from steps 1 and 3 as shown. Make two units measuring 2" × 2¾", including seam allowances.

Make 2 units,
2" × 2¾".

5. Sew together units from steps 2 and 4 to complete a block unit measuring 2¾" square, including seam allowances. Make two.

Make 2 units,
2¾" × 2¾".

6. In the same manner, make two block units with the dark and light pieces reversed as shown.

Make 2 units,
2¾" × 2¾".

7. Arrange the four block units, alternating the colors as shown. Sew the pieces together into rows. Join the rows to complete a block measuring 5" square, including seam allowances. Repeat to make 13 blocks.

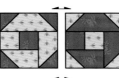
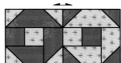 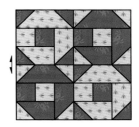

Make 13 blocks,
5" × 5".

Assembling and Finishing the Quilt

For more help with any of the finishing steps, go to ShopMartingale.com/HowtoQuilt.

1. Arrange the blocks and taupe 5" squares in five rows of five units each, alternating them as shown below. Sew the units together into rows; press. Sew the rows together, pressing after adding each row. The quilt top should measure 23" square, including seam allowances.

2. For the inner border, measure the length of the quilt top through the center and trim two tan 1¼"-wide strips to this measurement. Sew the strips to the sides of the quilt top and press the seam allowances toward the border.

3. Measure the width of the quilt top through the center, including the just-added border pieces, and trim the two remaining tan 1¼"-wide strips to this measurement. Sew the strips to the top and bottom of the quilt top and press the seam allowances toward the border.

4. For the outer border, repeat steps 2 and 3 using the blue-and-tan 4"-wide strips.

5. Layer the quilt top, batting, and backing. Baste the layers together and hand or machine quilt. The quilt shown is machine quilted with curved stitching in the pieced blocks and flower motifs in the plain alternate blocks. Feathers are quilted in the border.

6. Trim the excess batting and backing fabric. Use the blue 2"-wide strips to bind the quilt. Add a hanging sleeve, if desired, and a label.

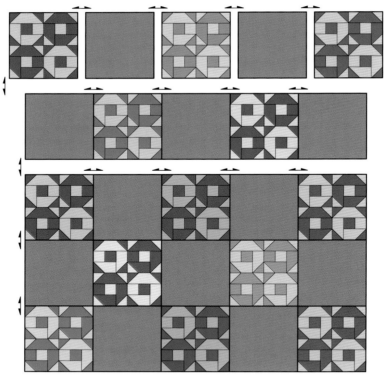

Quilt assembly

Battlefield Angel

Clara Barton, a nurse who treated soldiers injured on Civil War battlefields, later became famous when she established the American Red Cross. Her efforts are symbolized in the alternating Red Cross blocks of this quilt.

Materials

Yardage is based on 42"-wide fabric.

¼ yard *each* of 3 red prints for blocks

18 assorted dark scraps of blue, gray, and brown, at least 8" × 10" each, for blocks

18 assorted light scraps, at least 10" × 10" each, for blocks

⅝ yard of brown print for border

⅓ yard of dark brown print for binding

1⅜ yards of fabric for backing

40" × 50" piece of batting

To Add Interest

Select light and dark fabrics of differing values. Remember, a fabric only has to be lighter or darker than the other fabrics in each particular block.

Cutting

All measurements include ¼"-wide seam allowances.

From *each* of the red prints, cut:
24 rectangles, 1½" × 3½" (72 total)

From *each* of the dark scraps, cut:
21 squares, 1½" × 1½" (378 total; 13 are extra)

From *each* of the light scraps, cut:
21 squares, 1½" × 1½" (378 total; 8 are extra)
4 rectangles, 1½" × 3½" (72 total; 4 are extra)

From the brown print, cut:
4 strips, 4½" × 42"

From the dark brown print, cut:
5 strips, 2" × 42"

Battlefield Angel, pieced by Carol Hopkins and quilted by Sue Hellenbrand

Finished quilt size: 33½" × 43½" ◇ **Finished block size:** 5" × 5"

Making the A Blocks

Pair one light print with one dark print for each of the 17 blocks. Instructions are for making one block. Press the seam allowances as indicated by the arrows.

1. Sew together five matching dark 1½" squares and four matching light 1½" squares to make a nine-patch unit measuring 3½" square, including seam allowances.

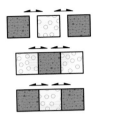

Make 1 unit,
3½" × 3½".

2. Sew two matching dark 1½" squares to opposite ends of a light 1½" × 3½" rectangle as shown. Press the dark squares toward the corners and trim the excess fabric to ¼" if desired. Make four units.

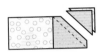 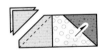

Make 4 units,
1½" × 3½".

3. Arrange four matching light 1½" squares and the units from steps 1 and 2 as shown. Sew the pieces together into rows, and then join the rows. Make 17 A blocks measuring 5½" square, including seam allowances.

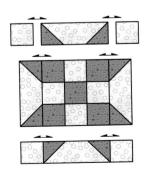 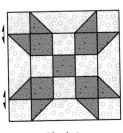

Block A.
Make 17 blocks,
5½" × 5½".

Making the B Blocks

Select a light print, a dark print, and a red print for each of the 18 blocks. Instructions are for making one block. Press the seam allowances as indicated by the arrows.

1. Sew together five matching light 1½" squares and four matching dark 1½" squares to make a nine-patch unit measuring 3½" square, including seam allowances.

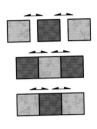

Make 1 unit,
3½" × 3½".

2. Sew light 1½" squares to opposite ends of a red 1½" × 3½" rectangle as shown. Press toward the corners and trim the excess fabric to ¼" if desired. Make four units.

Make 4 units,
1½" × 3½".

3. Arrange four dark 1½" squares and the units from steps 1 and 2 as shown. Sew the pieces together into rows, and then join the rows. Make 18 B blocks measuring 5½" square, including seam allowances.

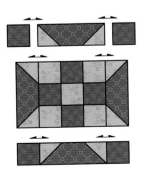 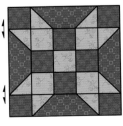

Block B.
Make 18 blocks,
5½" × 5½".

Assembling and Finishing the Quilt

For more help with any of the finishing steps, go to ShopMartingale.com/HowtoQuilt.

1. Arrange the A and B blocks as shown below. Sew the blocks together into rows and press. Sew the rows together, pressing after adding each row. The quilt top should measure 25½" × 35½", including seam allowances.

2. Measure the length of the quilt top through the center and trim two of the brown 4½"-wide strips to this measurement. Sew the strips to the sides of the quilt top.

3. Measure the width of the quilt top through the center, including the just-added border pieces, and trim the two remaining brown 4½"-wide strips to this measurement. Sew the strips to the top and bottom of the quilt top.

4. Layer the quilt top, batting, and backing. Baste the layers together and hand or machine quilt. The quilt shown is machine quilted in an allover meandering design.

5. Trim the excess batting and backing fabric. Use the dark brown 2"-wide strips to bind the quilt. Add a hanging sleeve, if desired, and a label.

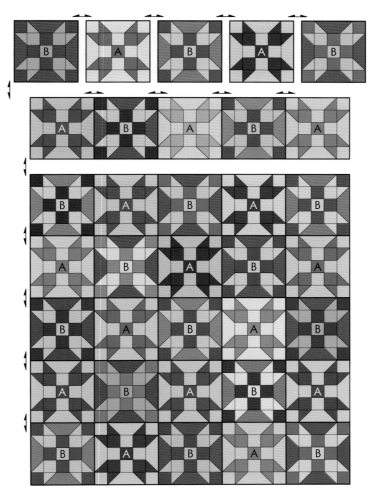

Quilt assembly

Patriotic Logs

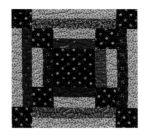

The antique quilt that provided inspiration for Patriotic Logs was constructed from flag bunting and was made by Amanda Beitler, a worker at the Collegeville Flag Factory in Pennsylvania.

Materials

Yardage is based on 42"-wide fabric.

⅞ yard of light print for blocks and sashing

⅛ yard *each* of 12 red prints for blocks and sashing

⅜ yard of blue print for blocks and sashing

¾ yard of red plaid for border and binding

1⅛ yards of fabric for backing

39" × 39" piece of batting

To Add Interest

Don't worry about trying to match shades of red. Select a variety of prints that include madder reds, brick reds, dark reds, pinkish reds, and red prints that contain other colors.

Cutting

All measurements include ¼"-wide seam allowances.

From the light print, cut:

24 strips, 1" × 42"

From *each* of the 12 red prints, cut:

2 strips, 1" × 42" (24 total)

From the blue print, cut:

3 strips, 1½" × 42"; crosscut into 72 squares, 1½" × 1½"

2 strips, 2½" × 42"; crosscut into 25 squares, 2½" × 2½"

From the red plaid, cut:

4 strips, 3½" × 42"

4 strips, 2" × 42"

Making the Blocks

This quilt is made from two slightly different blocks. All are made with the same red-and-light strip sets, but the five A blocks have the red fabric adjacent to the blue block centers, and the four B blocks have the light fabric adjacent to the blue centers. Alternating the color placement between the blocks allows the colors to alternate when the blocks are joined.

Press the seam allowances as indicated by the arrows.

1. Sew the red and light 1" × 42" strips together in pairs as shown to make 24 strip sets measuring 1½" × 42".

Make 24 strip sets, 1½" × 42".

2. From each *matching* pair of strip sets, cut:
   • 3 segments, 1½" × 2½" (36 total)
   • 3 segments, 1½" × 4½" (36 total)
   • 4 segments, 1½" × 6½" (48 total)

Little Treasures from Leftovers

Just as cooks find creative ways to use leftovers, quilters can, too. Cut 1" segments from the leftover red-and-light strip sets and sew them together in pairs to create little four patches. Sew the Four Patch blocks together with alternating blue 1½" squares for a patriotic table topper or with green 1½" squares for a holiday table mat.

Patriotic Logs, pieced by Carol Hopkins and quilted by Sue Hellenbrand
Finished quilt size: 32½" × 32½" ◇ **Finished block size:** 6" × 6"

3. Sort the segments from step 2 into 2½", 4½", and 6½" piles. As you sew these segments into blocks, use a variety of red fabrics in each block.

4. Sew pieced 1½" × 2½" segments to opposite sides of a blue 2½" square, with the red fabric touching the blue square. Make five units measuring 2½" × 4½", including seam allowances.

Make 5 units,
2½" × 4½".

5. Sew blue 1½" squares to opposite ends of a pieced 1½" × 2½" segment. Make 18 units measuring 1½" × 4½", including seam allowances.

Make 18 units,
1½" × 4½".

6. Sew units from step 5 to the top and bottom of a unit from step 4, with the red fabric touching the blue 2½" center square. This center unit should measure 4½" square, including seam allowances. Make five. Set aside the remaining pieced units from step 5.

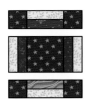

Make 5 units,
4½" × 4½".

7. Sew pieced 1½" × 4½" segments to opposite sides of the unit from step 6. Make five units measuring 4½" × 6½", including seam allowances.

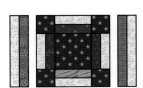 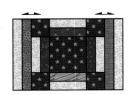

Make 5 units,
4½" × 6½".

8. Sew blue 1½" squares to opposite ends of a pieced 1½" × 4½" segment; press. Make 18 units measuring 1½" × 6½", including seam allowances.

Make 18 units,
1½" × 6½".

9. Sew units from step 8 to the top and bottom of a unit from step 7 to complete a block measuring 6½" square, including seam allowances. Make five A blocks.

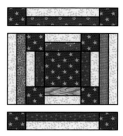 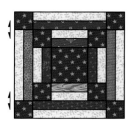

Block A.
Make 5 blocks,
6½" × 6½".

10. Follow step 4 to make four units but with the position of the red and light prints reversed. Proceed as before to make four B blocks using the remaining units from steps 2, 5, and 8, but with the light strips always positioned closest to the block centers.

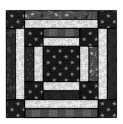

Block B.
Make 4 blocks,
6½" × 6½".

Making the Sashing Strips

Sew two different red-and-light 1½" × 6½" segments together to form a sashing unit measuring 2½" × 6½", including seam allowances. Make 24 sashing units.

Make 24 units,
2½" × 6½".

Assembling and Finishing the Quilt

For more help with any of the finishing steps, go to ShopMartingale.com/HowtoQuilt.

1. Arrange five A blocks, four B blocks, 24 sashing units, and 16 blue 2½" squares as shown below. Sew the pieces together into rows and press. Sew the rows together, pressing after adding each row.

2. Measure the length of the quilt top through the center and trim two red plaid 3½"-wide strips to this measurement. Sew the strips to the sides of the quilt and press the seam allowances toward the border.

3. Measure the width of the quilt top through the center, including the just-added border pieces, and trim the two remaining red plaid 3½"-wide strips to that length. Sew the strips to the top and bottom of the quilt and press the seam allowances toward the border.

4. Layer the quilt top, batting, and backing. Baste the layers together and hand or machine quilt. The quilt shown is machine quilted with an allover meandering pattern.

5. Trim the excess batting and backing fabric. Use the red plaid 2"-wide strips to bind the quilt. Add a hanging sleeve, if desired, and a label.

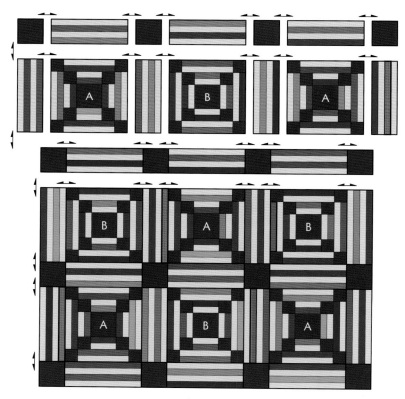

Quilt assembly

Streamers

Streamers were banner-like decorations attached to Army unit flags to denote extraordinary service in historic Civil War battles, often referred to as "campaigns." The names of battles were inscribed in the colors of the fighting units.

Materials

Yardage is based on 42"-wide fabric.

7 assorted light scraps, at least 10" × 10" each, for blocks

10 assorted medium or dark scraps, at least 10" × 12" each, for blocks

¾ yard of beige floral for setting triangles

1¼ yards of brown stripe OR ¼ yard of nondirectional brown print for setting strips

⅓ yard of blue print for inner border

1½ yards of gold print for outer border and binding

3 yards of fabric for backing

53" × 54" piece of batting

To Add Interest

If the stripe you like is wider than the pattern calls for, select an interesting portion of it and trim it to the width you need. If the stripe you like is narrower than the pattern calls for, cut multiple narrow stripes and sew them together. Don't forget to include seam allowances in your calculations.

Cutting

All measurements include ¼"-wide seam allowances.

From *each* of the light scraps, cut:
15 squares, 2⅛" × 2⅛"; cut in half diagonally to yield 30 triangles (210 total; 10 are extra)

From *each* of the medium or dark scraps, cut:
10 squares, 2⅛" × 2⅛"; cut in half diagonally to yield 20 triangles (200 total)
4 squares, 1¾" × 1¾" (40 total)
2 squares, 3" × 3" (20 total)

From the beige floral, cut:
2 strips, 8⅜" × 42"; crosscut into 8 squares, 8⅜" × 8⅜". Cut into quarters diagonally to yield 32 side triangles.
8 squares, 4½" × 4½"; cut in half diagonally to yield 16 corner triangles

From the *lengthwise* grain of the brown stripe, cut:*
3 strips, 2½" × 39"

From the blue print, cut:
4 strips, 2" × 42"

From the *lengthwise* grain of the gold print, cut:
4 strips, 5" × 48"
5 strips, 2" × 48"

If you're using a nondirectional print, cut the strips across the fabric width.

Streamers, pieced by Carol Hopkins and quilted by Lisa Ramsey

Finished quilt size: 46½" × 47⅞" ◇ **Finished block size:** 5" × 5"

Making the Blocks

Each block contains one light print and two different dark prints. For the ease of instructions we'll use dark triangles and medium block centers, but you can mix and match as desired. Instructions are for making one block. Press seam allowances as indicated by the arrows.

1. Sew light and dark 2⅛" triangles together in pairs to make 10 matching half-square-triangle units measuring 1¾" square, including seam allowances.

Make 10 units,
1¾" × 1¾".

2. Sew together three half-square-triangle units and a matching dark 1¾" square as shown. Make two units measuring 1¾" × 5½", including seam allowances.

Make 2 units,
1¾" × 5½".

3. Sew together two half-square-triangle units. Make two units measuring 1¾" × 3", including seam allowances.

Make 2 units,
1¾" × 3".

4. Arrange the units from steps 2 and 3 with a contrasting medium 3" square. Sew the pieces

into rows and then join the rows. Make 20 blocks measuring 5½" square, including seam allowances.

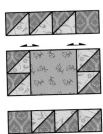 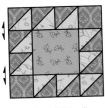

Make 20 blocks,
5½" × 5½".

Assembling and Finishing the Quilt

For more help with any of the finishing steps, go to ShopMartingale.com/HowtoQuilt.

1. Sew five blocks and eight beige floral 8⅜" triangles together as shown to make a row. Add beige floral 4½" triangles to the corners of the row and press. Make four rows that measure approximately 7½" × 35⅞", including seam allowances. Trim the rows if necessary, making sure to leave ¼" beyond the points of the blocks for seam allowance.

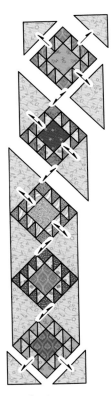

Make 4 rows,
7½" × 35⅞".

2. Measure the length of the rows in step 1 and trim the three brown-stripe strips to this measurement. Arrange the block rows and brown-stripe setting strips as shown below. Sew the block rows and strips together, pressing after adding each strip.

3. For the inner border, measure the length of the quilt top through the center and trim two blue 2"-wide strips to this measurement. Sew the strips to the sides of the quilt and press the seam allowances toward the border.

4. Measure the width of the quilt top through the center, including the just-added border pieces, and trim the two remaining blue 2"-wide strips to this measurement. Sew the strips to the top and bottom of the quilt and press the seam allowances toward the border.

5. Repeat steps 3 and 4 with the gold 5"-wide strips to make the outer border.

6. Layer the quilt top, batting, and backing. Baste the layers together and hand or machine quilt. The quilt shown is machine quilted with a flower motif in each block and a wide feather in the outer border. The sashing strips are quilted following the curving lines in the fabric.

7. Trim the excess batting and backing fabric. Use the gold 2"-wide strips to bind the quilt. Add a hanging sleeve, if desired, and a label.

Quilt assembly

Fireballs

As the Civil War dragged on, many families experienced a shortage of coal to warm their homes. It's been reported that Southerners burned mixtures of coal dust, sawdust, sand, and wet clay formed into hardened lumps to provide heat.

Materials

Yardage is based on 42"-wide fabric.

¼ yard of light print for blocks

12 assorted red scraps, at least 4" × 6" each, for blocks

12 assorted black or brown scraps, at least 4" × 6" each, for blocks

1⅛ yards of red stripe OR ¼ yard of nondirectional red print for sashing

⅓ yard of black print for cornerstones and binding

¾ yard of black-and-red print for border

1 yard of fabric for backing

30" × 35" piece of batting

To Add Interest

Don't be afraid to use large-scale prints in small blocks. Notice how much color and movement they add to the blocks in this little quilt.

Cutting

All measurements include ¼"-wide seam allowances.

From the light print, cut:

2 strips, 1⅞" × 42"; crosscut into 24 squares, 1⅞" × 1⅞". Cut squares in half diagonally to yield 48 triangles

2 strips, 1½" × 42"; crosscut into 48 squares, 1½" × 1½"

From *each* of the red scraps, cut:

2 rectangles, 1½" × 2½" (24 total)

1 square, 1⅞" × 1⅞"; cut in half diagonally to yield 2 triangles (24 total)

From *each* of the black or brown scraps, cut:

2 rectangles, 1½" × 2½" (24 total)

1 square, 1⅞" × 1⅞"; cut in half diagonally to yield 2 triangles (24 total)

From the *lengthwise* grain of the red stripe, cut:

31 rectangles, 1½" × 4½", centering the same design in each strip

From the black print, cut:

3 strips, 2" × 42"

20 squares, 1½" × 1½"

From the *lengthwise* grain of the black-and-red print, cut:*

2 strips, 3½" × 22"

From the *crosswise* grain of the remaining black-and-red print, cut:*

2 strips, 3½" × 24"

*If you're using nondirectional fabric, you can cut all strips across the width of the fabric.

Making the Blocks

Each block uses one red print, one black print, and one light print. Instructions are for making one block. Press the seam allowances as indicated by the arrows.

1. Sew together light and red 1⅞" triangles to make two matching half-square-triangle units, and make two black-and-light units in the same manner. Each half-square-triangle unit should measure 1½" square, including seam allowances.

Make 2 of each,
1½" × 1½".

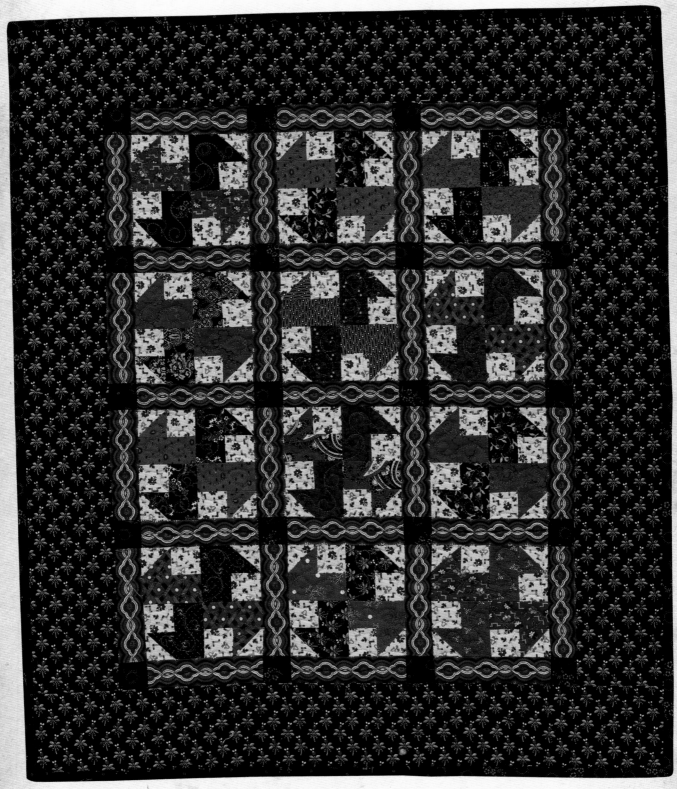

Fireballs, pieced by Carol Hopkins and quilted by Lisa Ramsey

Finished quilt size: 22½" × 27½" ◇ **Finished block size:** 4" × 4"

2. Sew a light 1½" square to the right edge of each unit from step 1. The unit should measure 1½" × 2½", including seam allowances. Make two units of each colorway.

Make 2 of each,
1½" × 2½".

3. Sew a matching red 1½" × 2½" rectangle to the bottom of each red unit and a black rectangle to each black unit; press. Make two of each. The units should measure 2½" square, including seam allowances.

Make 2 of each,
2½" × 2½".

4. Arrange two matching red units and two matching black units from step 3 as shown. Sew the pieces into rows and then sew the rows together to make a block measuring 4½" square, including seam allowances. Repeat to make 12 blocks.

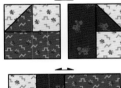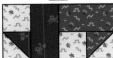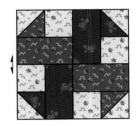

Make 12 blocks,
4½" × 4½".

Assembling and Finishing the Quilt

For more help with any of the finishing steps, go to ShopMartingale.com/HowtoQuilt.

1. Arrange the blocks, the red-stripe sashing rectangles, and the black print cornerstones as shown. Sew the pieces into rows; press. Sew the rows together, pressing after adding each row.

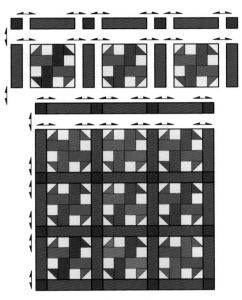

Quilt assembly

2. Measure the length of the quilt top through the center and trim the black-and-red 3½"-wide strips *cut from the lengthwise grain* to this measurement. Sew the strips to the sides of the quilt and press the seam allowances toward the border.

3. Measure the width of the quilt top through the center, including the just-added border pieces, and trim the two remaining black-and-red 3½"-wide strips to this measurement. Sew the strips to the top and bottom of the quilt and press the seam allowances toward the border.

4. Layer the quilt top, batting, and backing. Baste the layers together and hand or machine quilt. The quilt shown is machine quilted with a swirl through each red section and each black section of the blocks and a feather design in the border.

5. Trim the excess batting and backing fabric. Use the black 2"-wide strips to bind the quilt. Add a hanging sleeve, if desired, and a label.

From 1861 to 1865, more than 8,000 instances of hostilities occurred across 23 states. Major battles, such as Gettysburg, Antietam, Bull Run, and Shiloh, were part of organized campaigns that had an impact on the direction, duration, conduct, and outcome of the Civil War.

Materials

Yardage is based on 42"-wide fabric.

11" × 11" scrap of light gray print for blocks
7" × 9" scrap of tan print for block background
8 assorted light scraps, at least 5" × 5" each, for blocks
8 assorted dark scraps of red, blue, gray, and brown, at least 5" × 6" each, for blocks
9" × 12" scrap of dark brown floral for blocks
3" × 5" scrap of pink check for blocks
¼ yard of taupe floral for outer border
¼ yard of taupe vine print for binding
⅔ yard of fabric for backing
24" × 24" piece of batting

To Add Interest

Select a background fabric for the Star block that is similar in color and value to the outer border; this will help showcase the flying geese encircling the quilt center.

Cutting

All measurements include ¼"-wide seam allowances.

From the light gray scrap, cut:
16 squares, 2" × 2"
8 squares, 1¼" × 1¼"

From the tan scrap, cut:
4 rectangles, 2" × 3½"
4 squares, 2" × 2"

From *each* of the light scraps, cut:
4 squares, 2" × 2" (32 total)

From *each* of the dark scraps, cut:
2 rectangles, 2" × 3½" (16 total)

From *each of 4* of the dark scraps, cut:
1 rectangle, 1¼" × 2" (4 total)

From the dark brown floral, cut:
4 squares, 3½" × 3½"
8 squares, 2" × 2"

From the pink check scrap, cut:
2 rectangles, 1¼" × 3½"

From the taupe floral, cut:
2 strips, 3" × 42"; cut in half crosswise to yield 4 strips, 3" × 21"

From the taupe vine print, cut:
2 strips, 2" × 42"

Campaign, pieced by Carol Hopkins and quilted by Lisa Ramsey

Finished quilt size: 17½" × 17½" ◇ Finished block size: 6" × 6"

Making the Block

Press all seam allowances as indicated by the arrows.

1. Make a small flying-geese unit with two light gray 1¼" squares and one dark 1¼" × 2" rectangle as shown. Make four. In the same manner, make four large flying-geese units using the tan 2" × 3½" rectangles and the dark brown floral 2" squares.

Make 4 units,
1¼" × 2".

Make 4 units,
2" × 3½".

2. Join the small flying-geese units in a row to make the Star block center, 2" × 3½".

Make 1 unit,
2" × 3½".

3. Sew pink check 1¼" × 3½" rectangles to opposite sides of the flying-geese unit to make a center unit measuring 3½" square, including seam allowances.

Make 1 center unit,
3½" × 3½".

4. Arrange the center unit, large flying-geese units, and four tan 2" squares as shown. Sew the pieces together into rows and then join the rows to complete a Star block measuring 6½" square, including seam allowances.

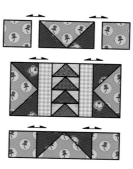 
Make 1 block,
6½" × 6½".

Making the Pieced Border Units

1. Make a large flying-geese unit with two light 2" squares and one dark 2" × 3½" rectangle. Make 16 units and then sew them into four strips of four flying-geese units each. Press the seam allowances open.

2. Sew a light gray 2" square to each corner of a dark brown floral 3½" square to make a Square-in-a-Square block. Make four blocks.

Make 4 blocks,
3½" × 3½".

Assembling and Finishing the Quilt

For more help with any of the finishing steps, go to ShopMartingale.com/HowtoQuilt.

1. Sew flying-geese border strips to opposite sides of the Star block, noting that the geese should point around the Star block in a clockwise fashion. Sew a Square-in-a-Square block to each end of the remaining flying-geese strips, and sew these strips to the top and bottom of the Star block.

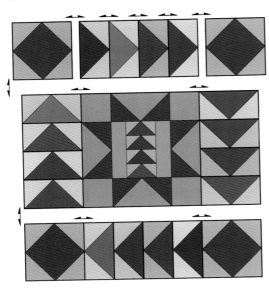

Quilt assembly

2. Measure the length of the quilt top through the center and trim two of the taupe floral 3"-wide strips to this measurement. Sew the strips to the sides of the quilt top.

3. Measure the width of the quilt through the center, including the just-added border pieces, and trim the two remaining taupe floral 3"-wide strips to this measurement. Sew the strips to the top and bottom of the quilt top.

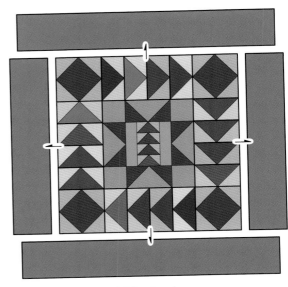

Adding borders

4. Layer the quilt top, batting, and backing. Baste the layers together and hand or machine quilt. The quilt shown is machine quilted with a pair of leaves and a swirl in each large flying-geese unit, the center star is quilted with curving lines from one point to the next in the triangles, and the border is quilted with a modified feather design.

5. Trim the excess batting and backing fabric. Use the taupe vine print 2"-wide strips to bind the quilt. Add a hanging sleeve, if desired, and a label.

Gingerbread

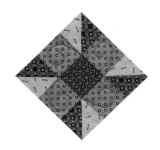

Gingerbread was a comfort food given to sick and wounded soldiers in field hospitals. The diary of one Civil War nurse referred to it as "a singular food for sick men." The shades of brown in this quilt bring to mind the toasty color of gingerbread.

Materials

Yardage is based on 42"-wide fabric.

18 assorted light scraps, at least 3" × 6" *each*, for blocks

18 assorted dark scraps of red, blue, brown, and black, at least 6" × 6" *each*, for blocks

18 assorted cheddar scraps, at least 5" × 5" *each*, for blocks

⅓ yard of brown stripe for sashing

⅛ yard of tan print for cornerstones

⅓ yard of tan stripe for setting triangles

¼ yard of cheddar-and-red print for inner border

¾ yard of brown-and-cheddar print for outer border and binding

1¼ yards of fabric for backing

38" × 45" piece of batting

To Add Interest

Substitute orange and gold prints for the cheddar pieces in a few of the blocks.

Cutting

All measurements include ¼"-wide seam allowances.

From *each* of the light scraps, cut:

2 squares, 2⅜" × 2⅜"; cut in half diagonally to yield 4 triangles (72 total)

From *each* of the dark scraps, cut:

2 squares, 2⅜" × 2⅜"; cut in half diagonally to yield 4 triangles (72 total)

1 square, 2" × 2" (18 total)

From *each* of the cheddar scraps, cut:

4 squares, 2" × 2" (72 total)

From the brown stripe, cut:

6 strips, 1½" × 42"; crosscut into 48 rectangles, 1½" × 5"

From the tan print, cut:

31 squares, 1½" × 1½"

From the tan stripe, cut:

3 squares, 7¾" × 7¾"; cut into quarters diagonally to yield 12 side triangles (2 are extra)

2 squares, 4¼" × 4¼"; cut in half diagonally to yield 4 corner triangles*

From the cheddar-and-red print, cut:

4 strips, 1¼" × 42"

From the brown-and-cheddar print, cut:

4 strips, 3½" × 42"

4 strips, 2" × 42"

*If you want the stripe to run in the same direction in all of the corner triangles, cut the squares in half as shown in the diagram below.

 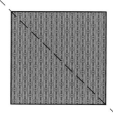

Cut one of the squares in one direction, and one in the opposite direction.

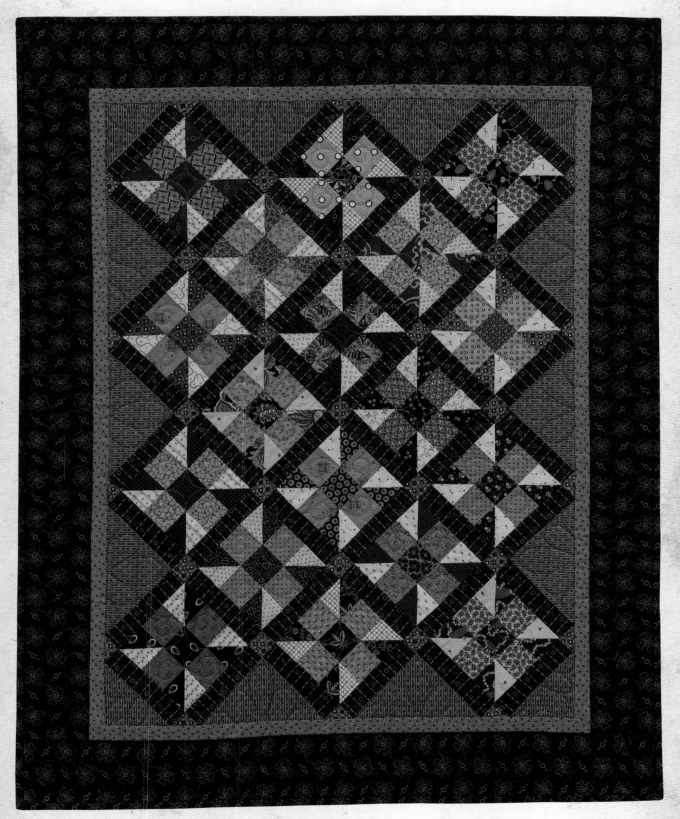

Gingerbread, pieced by Carol Hopkins and quilted by Lisa Ramsey

Finished quilt size: 31¼" × 39" ◇ **Finished block size:** 4½" × 4½"

Making the Blocks

Each block contains one cheddar print, one light print, and one dark print. Instructions are for making one block. Press all seam allowances as indicated by the arrows.

1. Sew together light and dark 2⅜" triangles to make four matching half-square-triangle units measuring 2" square, including seam allowances.

Make 4 units,
2" × 2".

2. Arrange the four half-square-triangle units, a matching dark 2" square, and four matching cheddar 2" squares as shown. Sew the pieces together into rows, and then join the rows to complete a block measuring 5" square, including seam allowances. Make 18 blocks.

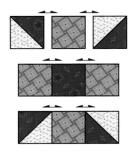 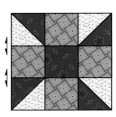

Make 18 blocks,
5" × 5".

Assembling and Finishing the Quilt

For more help with any of the finishing steps, go to ShopMartingale.com/HowtoQuilt.

1. Arrange the blocks, brown-striped sashing rectangles, and tan-striped cornerstones into diagonal rows as shown in the quilt assembly diagram above right. Add the tan side triangles and corner triangles.

2. Sew the blocks and sashing rectangles into diagonal rows as shown above right. Then join cornerstones and sashing rectangles to make sashing strips. Press the seam allowances open.

3. Sew the block and sashing rows together, pressing the seam allowances open after adding each row. Add the corner triangles and press the seam allowances toward the triangles.

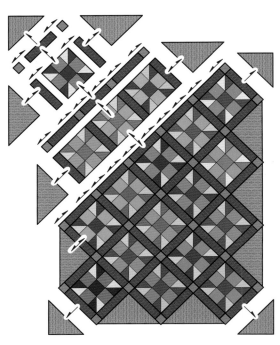

Quilt assembly

4. Trim the quilt top, leaving a ¼" seam allowance beyond the centers of the cornerstones.

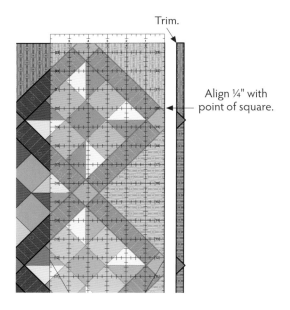

Trim.

Align ¼" with point of square.

5. For the inner border, measure the length of the quilt top through the center and trim two of the cheddar 1¼"-wide strips to this measurement. Sew the strips to the sides of the quilt and press the seam allowances toward the border.

6. Measure the width of the quilt top through the center, including the just-added border pieces, and trim the two remaining cheddar 1¼"-wide strips to this measurement. Sew the strips to the top and bottom of the quilt and press the seam allowances toward the border.

7. For the outer border, repeat steps 5 and 6 using the brown-and-cheddar 3½"-wide strips.

8. Layer the quilt top, batting, and backing. Baste the layers together and hand or machine quilt. The quilt shown is machine quilted with a swirling flower in each block. The sashing pieces around each block are quilted in a curvy-edge circle. The outer border is quilted with feathers.

9. Trim the excess batting and backing fabric. Use the brown-and-cheddar 2"-wide strips to bind the quilt. Add a hanging sleeve, if desired, and a label.

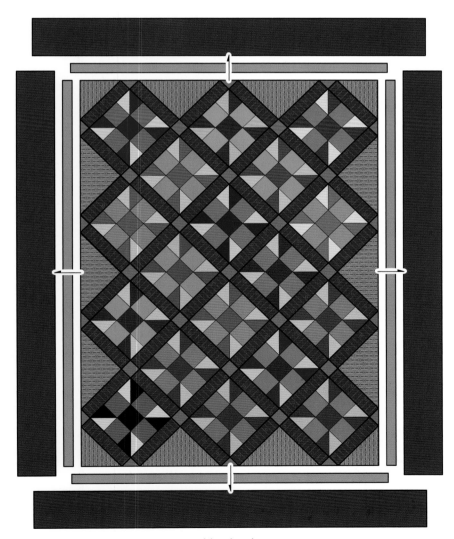

Adding borders

About the Author

Carol Hopkins, recently retired from a 40-year teaching career at Purdue University, enjoys spending time with her husband, her children and their spouses, and her four grandchildren at her home in West Lafayette, Indiana. This, her fifth publication with Martingale since 2012, follows the success of three best-selling "Civil War Legacies" books and *The 4" × 5" Quilt Block Anthology: 182 Blocks for Reproduction Fabrics*. Carol creates six to eight new patterns each year marketed as "Civil War Legacies" and "Vintage Legacies," each of which contains dozens of eighteenth- or nineteenth-century reproduction prints. Carol's books and patterns are sold worldwide, and many of her designs have been featured in national and international quilt publications. To learn more about Carol and see further examples of her work, visit CarolHopkinsDesigns.com.

Acknowledgments

This book wouldn't exist without the efforts of many people. First, I thank all of the editors, the fabulous photographer Brent Kane, and everyone on the marketing and production staffs at Martingale, for turning a pile of quilts and a computer disk of instructions into a lovely finished product. I feel so fortunate to have been able to work with this talented group of professionals on another book.

Special thanks to Lisa Ramsey, machine quilter extraordinaire, for the creative designs she fits into little blocks, for her amazing feather borders, and for her willingness to rearrange her life on short notice to help me meet deadlines. I also thank Sue Hellenbrand for her quilting of small meandering designs on two of the quilts.

I greatly appreciate the opportunity to work with fabrics from newly released collections provided by Pati Violick (Marcus Fabrics), Laura Jaquinto (Windham Fabrics), Carrie Nelson and Lissa Alexander (Moda Fabrics), and Edyta Sitar (Andover Fabrics). Thank you for your generosity.

Many thanks to Tim, Emily, and Mike for not complaining when you come to visit and discover that your old bedrooms currently resemble storage units. If only the quilts were big enough to sleep under!

My biggest thanks, as always, go to my parents, Anne and Bill Horgan, who nurtured my exploration of new pathways. I miss you every day.